BORDER CROSSINGS

BORDER CROSSINGS

US Culture and Education in Saskatchewan, 1905–1937

KERRY ALCORN

McGill-Queen's University Press

Montreal & Kingston • London • Ithaca

ISBN 978-0-7735-4287-7 (cloth)
ISBN 978-0-7735-4288-4 (paper)
ISBN 978-0-7735-9003-8 (ePDF)
ISBN 978-0-7735-9004-5 (ePUB)

Legal deposit fourth quarter 2013
Bibliothèque nationale du Québec

Printed in Canada on acid-free paper that is 100% ancient forest free (100% post-consumer recycled), processed chlorine free

McGill-Queen's University Press acknowledges the support of the Canada Council for the Arts for our publishing program. We also acknowledge the financial support of the Government of Canada through the Canada Book Fund for our publishing activities.

Library and Archives Canada Cataloguing in Publication

Alcorn, Kerry, 1962-, author
Border crossings : US culture and education in Saskatchewan, 1905-1937
/ Kerry Alcorn.

Includes bibliographical references and index. Issued in print and electronic formats.
ISBN 978-0-7735-4287-7 (bound). – ISBN 978-0-7735-4288-4 (pbk.). –
ISBN 978-0-7735-9003-8 (ePDF). – ISBN 978-0-7735-9004-5 (ePUB)

1. Education – Saskatchewan – American influences – History – 20th century.
2. Education and state – Saskatchewan – History – 20th century. 3. Education – Saskatchewan – Philosophy – History – 20th century. 4. Comparative education. 5. Great Plains – History. I. Title.
LA418.S3A43 2013   370.9712409›041   C2013-906758-2   C2013-906759-0

Contents

Tables and Figures

TABLES

FIGURES

PART ONE

Transferring US Culture

◇◇◇◇◇◇

1

◇◇◇◇◇◇

Introduction
The Continental West

HEADING WEST, TRAVERSING THE AMERICAN MIDWEST AND GREAT Plains by car from Kentucky to Saskatchewan, I finally come to a place where I begin to feel at home, although I am still eighteen hours' drive from my residence in Saskatoon. This place is where Interstate 80, which runs east and west across Iowa, gives way to Interstate 680 and meets Interstate 29 heading north, some 60 miles north of Omaha, Nebraska. Here the lightly rolling terrain, the world's largest truck stop, and factory outlets nestling among seemingly endless rows of corn recede into the rear-view mirror, and I find before me what I have not seen for some time: the far distant horizon, bright blue sky, and flatness as far as I can see. Here I breathe a sigh of relief as the north–south flow of traffic dwindles to a trickle in comparison to the torrent that moves from east to west across the continent. Not far north in South Dakota, I find my first native-run casino and rows of soybeans – things familiar to me. Further still into North Dakota, I catch sight of wheat fields, the Canadian National Railways, and, finally, grasslands. Here, as I travel north adjacent to the Missouri River valley, I feel the comfort of what I know as prairie. It was not always this way for me. It would take a half-dozen migrations between Saskatoon and Lexington over a six-year period before I could articulate what I now see as obvious.

When my family and I first moved to the United States in 1997, little did I realize we were about to live the process of cultural transfer. My wife had accepted a position as a doctoral student at the University of Kentucky in Lexington, there to study pharmaceutical sciences under some of the finest scholars in the field. Moving south in late August, we passed through the familiar surroundings of Estevan, Saskatchewan, earlier than we had expected, unable to find accommodations. Provincial baseball championships had claimed every hotel and motel room in town.

The border crossing itself went without incident. The US Immigration and Naturalization Service official welcomed us warmly. He chuckled when I asked if there were any hotels in Portal, North Dakota, population approximately 50. His skin was pinkish, the hair on his head and arms a bright orange. His nametag betrayed his Scandinavian roots. Nothing of this was out of the ordinary. His sidearm, however, spoke of a different land than the one I left behind. The flag flying outside his port of entry was familiar enough, but seemed somehow unusual that night, as did the smiling photo of President Clinton on the office wall. As I recall it now, everything seemed different to me. Even the thunderstorms in the distance – a common occurrence in Saskatchewan – appeared somehow more dangerous; more forbidding. The following day we ate lunch in Devil's Lake, North Dakota. The waitress there offered us gravy on our meals. This somewhat bewildered us; we thanked her but declined. The next morning we arrived in Sioux City, Iowa, to learn that tornadoes had alighted in the county – a threat new to us. Stores offered us "sacks" instead of bags, we drank iced tea that was simply tea with ice in it, and we could not stop sweating from the humidity. For me, our first move from the bald Canadian prairie of Saskatchewan through the American plains and Midwest was a trip into a foreign land. These foreign qualities, I would learn, existed entirely within my own mind.

Because of my academic background in international relations, this foreignness did not surprise me. Within that field of study, you learn that international borders, whether man-made or natural, recognize and divide pre-existing difference. Similarly, histories of Canada, and indeed those of the continent generally, speak of movement in terms largely of east to west, paying scant attention to the north–south flow of culture beyond the migration of bison and some First Nations peoples across the continental plains.

By the time I returned to Lexington for the second time in 1999, now as a student, I studied international relations or Canadian history no longer, but American history and the history of education in the United States. I also read in the broad fields of cultural and postmodern history and dabbled in the quintessentially American pragmatic philosophy of Richard Rorty and John Dewey. Such an exposure transformed my thinking about a variety of topics, especially in the field of education. Not until my return to Saskatoon in 2000, however, when I began to read the history of Canadian education, did this change in thinking caramelize into the story that follows. On reading several "standard" histories of Canadian education, I quickly discovered that I had heard this story before. After all, is it not the case that Egerton Ryerson, the patriarch of English-Canadian education, was simply a later, Anglicized version of Horace Mann, the patriarch of American education?

EDUCATION IN THE WEST

Very few book-length histories of Canadian education pay heed to the evolution of education in Canada's west. Because scholars from Ontario write the vast majority of them, this is perhaps not surprising. If they mention education in Saskatchewan or Alberta, they do so usually as an afterthought, late in a chapter near the end of an encyclopaedic and rather dull description of educational development in Ontario and Quebec. Take, for example, Alison Prentice, who invokes Seymour Martin Lipset to argue that differences in education between Canada and the United States reflect divergent political cultures. Prentice warns, "There is no such thing as an American system of education." Despite arguing that Canadian education makes little sense without reference to the American model, Prentice does conclude that its history is different, because Canada developed later and evolved more slowly. "When the English did come in numbers to Canada, they were often the products not of a quest for a revolutionary new society, but of a counter-revolutionary preference for traditional patterns."[1]

Prentice's argument relies on Lipset's later work, which emphasizes the inherent contrasts between the two countries' political cultures. This stance was quite at odds with his initial study of political culture in Saskatchewan, which he viewed as very similar to US Midwestern and Great Plains political orientations. Lipset's first book was the culmination of his doctoral dissertation and 50 years later remains the quintessential examination of Saskatchewan's political culture. In accepting Lipset's later interpretation of Canadian political culture, Prentice assumes a capacious view of English-Canadian education – one reflecting an Anglo-Celtic majority. If the historian interprets Saskatchewan's political culture to be different from the American, then one expects divergent patterns of education. If, as I hope to show, evidence suggests that Saskatchewan's political culture is closely akin to American forms, particularly those in the Midwest and Plains, then one can expect the development of schooling for grades from kindergarten to grade 12 (K–12) in Saskatchewan to parallel that to the south.[2]

The few existing histories of Saskatchewan's education are anthologies of collected papers and offer little on the broad ebb and flow of educational movements. These volumes tend to focus on the experience of particular ethnic or religious groups, such as Mennonites or Hutterites, at a time when foreign settlement reached its zenith. Fresh from my Kentucky readings of the "gold standard" histories of American education from the likes of Lawrence Cremin and Herbert Kliebard, I found myself wanting more from my own country's and, needless to say, province's historians of education. I discovered it in the work of George S. Tomkins.

Tomkins's crowning achievement as a historian of the Canadian curriculum is *A Common Countenance: Stability and Change in the Canadian Curriculum*, which he researched and wrote while on faculty at the University of British Columbia.

For Tomkins, the history of the Canadian curriculum bears the face of the Anglo-Celtic majority and pays homage to Protestant and British cultural norms while resisting American hegemony. For minorities, particularly Roman Catholic French Canadians, cultural survival meant resistance to the cultural norms of this dominant culture.

Writing a history of education for a country so large and diverse as Canada is a challenge, and one that Tomkins met with great balance and acumen. He provided the regional and provincial balance I found so lacking in all other "national" histories of education. On a national scale, his interpretation is most certainly accurate. For Saskatchewan, however, his titular "common countenance" looks to me like the face of "Uncle Sam." The Anglo-Celtic majority, so central to his argument at a national level, never existed in Saskatchewan between 1905 and 1937, the focus of my study. In Saskatchewan, minorities did seek to resist Anglo-Celtic dominance and chose the rural school, both in its makeup and its governance, as the most obvious and democratic instrument within which to resist.

In the field of education from kindergarten through grade 12, Saskatchewan felt American influence in a variety of ways between 1905 and 1930. In 1905, the year it became a province, it was very short of trained teachers. Teachers with US training helped meet this need. Similarly, the lack of an indigenous textbook industry led to dependence on other sources. While Ontario produced texts, these were often more expensive and of lower quality than US publications. Much like the histories I would read a century later, Canadian textbooks paid little heed to the frontier or settlement experiences of prairie residents. American textbooks did so, but within a Midwestern or Plains context. Canadian prairie educators often pursued graduate study in American universities and returned home sporting US ideas and innovations. This was especially the case during the Progressive age of education reform (roughly from 1890 through the early 1950s), whose language Saskatchewan policy makers adopted and adapted. The ease with which American experts in education, and the programs and curricula they produced, crossed into Canada also eased the reception of US culture and practice.

The reliance by Saskatchewan's policy makers on American education practice is obvious in the area of K–12 schooling, yet even greater in higher education. The story of the University of Saskatchewan from its creation in 1907 until the first president retired in 1937 is the tale of one person's influence on the institution – Walter C. Murray. Though a native New Brunswicker and a graduate of the University of Edinburgh, Murray was to fashion a truly American university on the banks of the South Saskatchewan River. Patterning itself after the "idea" of the University of Wisconsin in Madison, borrowing its "Collegiate Gothic" architecture from Washington University in St Louis, Missouri, and employing a large percentage of American or US-trained professors, the University of Saskatchewan was the first institution of its kind in Canada, but it resembled several Midwest universities. Throughout his tenure as president of the University of Saskatchewan, Murray relied on American models of higher education and pined for US sources of funding, including that provided by the Carnegie Foundation for the Advancement of Teaching (CFAT) and the Rockefeller Foundation. Similarly, when questions of academic freedom arose, he invoked decisions from high-profile cases in the United States. Murray's university epitomized an American-style land grant university, with the study of agriculture at its core.

To suggest that Canadian education is beholden to its American counterpart challenges the historiography of both Canada and its education. Both fields maintain that Canadian culture moved from east to west and was predominantly British in origin. Much like the automobile traffic I experienced crossing the American Midwest and Plains, the story moves mainly east and west, with only a trickle going north and south. To argue that the core of Canadian culture about 1900 was anything other than British would clearly be capricious, but it would be worthwhile, I maintain, to explore the influence of American culture, particularly on the prairies and specifically on Saskatchewan. In this regard, I wish to focus on the extent to which prairie culture, and education policy in Saskatchewan especially, resembled that emanating from the American Midwest and Plains. Like Daniel T. Rodgers, I intend to look first for similarities rather than for differences.[3]

The settlement of what became the provinces of Alberta and Saskatchewan was an extension of the same process in the US Midwest and Plains. It occurred some 15 to 20 years later but followed a very similar pattern and produced similar results. US settlers followed free land in the quest for a piece of the American dream. When free land disappeared about 1900 on the American frontier, the Canadian government quickly took advantage and, through advertising and recruitment, lured settlers into what was until 1905 the Northwest Territories. Unlike in the US context, however, where private business interests attempted to settle for profit, in Canada the federal government was the impetus behind settlement.

The number of US citizens who entered the Northwest Territories and later Saskatchewan and Alberta is difficult to establish – perhaps 1¼ million between 1890 and 1924.[4] Some of these newcomers were expatriate Canadians, while others were Europeans who had stopped briefly in the United States on their way north. A large portion, however, were Americans born and raised. Large-scale migration from the American Midwest and Plains helped shape the culture of Saskatchewan and directly affected its education starting with its formation in 1905.

Paul Sharp, an American historian who studied agrarian revolt in western Canada, captures well the relationship between the northern and southern plains: "The influence of identical environments was reinforced by the ease with which men and ideas crossed the international boundary to the north. The impact of the American republic has been great upon life in every section of the dominion, but nowhere is it more pronounced than in the Canadian West. The American farmers who helped to settle that vast region carried with them an agrarian experience which had matured under the stimuli of similar conditions in the American West. Typically western ideas quickly took root in the prairie provinces, where, combined with eastern Canadian and British traditions, they flowered in an agrarian revolt that recalls the earlier Populist crusade and parallels the contemporary agrarian movements in the American Northwest."[5]

Historians have analysed the influence of British culture on western Canada, and that of eastern Canada as well. The history I wish to tell, however, focuses on the degree of American influence on Saskatchewan. My goal is not to reject or replace what they have written, but to provide an alternative way to think about the province's history, particularly vis-à-vis education policy in both K–12 and higher education. In so doing, I seek to avoid suggesting that my history is correct and those that precede it, incorrect. Instead, as Richard Rorty has stated eloquently, I wish simply to redirect the conversation about the history of Saskatchewan's education policy.[6]

What follows then is a history of the extent to which American culture and educational policy penetrated Saskatchewan between 1905 and about 1937. I discuss how American culture – which William H. Sewell, Jr, defines as *meanings* and *practice* – moved north across the forty-ninth parallel.[7] Cultural transfer occurred through the movement of people, through the free flow of publications such as books, newspapers, and various technical journals, and through a host of mechanisms, including Canadians studying in the United States. The inherent mistrust and resistance to most things emanating from Canada's east, which agrarian revolt strengthened, produced a vacuum for inspiration among Saskatchewan's policy makers. American innovation often filled this void.[8] Through the combining factors of cultural transfer and anti-eastern sentiment, policy makers accustomed themselves to looking south for inspiration rather than east, as many Canadian commentators previously suggested. The meaning of government, schools, the east, and the land itself took on a very American connotation.

The underlying spirit behind this history is that of American pragmatism. As Alan Wolfe suggests, "A suspicion of demarcations is part of pragmatism's appeal, especially to those persuaded that the more powerful the boundary, the more likely its arbitrary construction and ultimate unjustifiability."[9] While Wolfe is most assuredly referring to many types of boundaries, I attend first to the one along the forty-ninth parallel.

THREE SCHOOLS OF HISTORICAL ANALYSIS

In uncovering parallel developments in culture and education across the North American Great Plains, I position myself clearly in one of three camps of historical analysis of the Canadian and American wests, which Thomas D. Isern and R. Bruce Shepard describe as *continentalist, comparative*, and *borderlands*.[10] Continentalists, they argue, perceive a regional integrity and identity to the continental Great Plains, especially vis-à-vis the study of history, agriculture, and, as I hope to show, education policy. People observe the international border, but it had little influence on the region's historical development. In seeking cross-border cultural affinity in a fashion similar to American historians Walter Prescott Webb and the initial work of Paul F. Sharp, but also the early writing of American political sociologist Seymour Martin Lipset, I am unabashedly a continentalist.

Yet both Sharp and Lipset, after publishing their graduate fieldwork on Canada's west, moved towards a more comparative approach. For Isern and Shepard, scholars who seek comparison expose national distinctions, attributing greater import to the boundary than a continental approach. Lipset's cumulative work on comparative political cultures, *Continental Divide*, necessarily assumes a capacious view of Canadian and American political cultures, inevitably blending the unique culture of the prairie and Plains regions into their respective national political cultures. Because of his new emphasis on the political culture of Canada's east following his release of *Agrarian Socialism*, Saskatchewan quickly loses its distinctive political culture within a wider English-Canadian counterrevolutionary spirit that he sees as deferential to authority and monarchy. I tend to think that both Lipset and Sharp got it "right" the first time – *Agrarian Socialism* wedded cross-border cultural affinities, and Sharp viewed agrarian revolt and protest as a singular, transnational movement unaffected by an international boundary. Lipset's gaze later broadens beyond the region, while Sharp's narrows within it.

Sharp's outstanding *Whoop-Up Country*, about the furthest western continental Plains along the Whoop-Up Trail linking Fort Benton, Montana, and Fort McLeod, Alberta, is comparative in nature. Unlike his continentalist *Agrarian Revolt*, the trail symbolized for him peaceful American cultural penetration into westernmost Alberta, "draining" the surrounding hinterland of its wealth, and depositing it at the cosmopolitan frontier town of Fort Benton.[11] In *Whoop-Up Country*, nationalism gave reality to the forty-ninth parallel, replacing a north–south axis of regional interdependence with an east–west axis of discrete, national economic and political development.[12]

Sharp pinpoints the sea change to 1883 – the very year the Canadian Pacific Railway reached Medicine Hat in southeastern soon-to-be Alberta. Regional populations spanning the border quickly lost their unity and identity. Parallel developments "were born of similar geographic, climatic, cultural, and economic environments, not of conscious imitation or adaptation."[13] My argument asserts, much in contrast to Sharp's here, that Saskatchewan policy makers for both K–12 and higher education indeed imitated and adapted American Great Plains solutions to their Saskatchewan prairie problems.

But how might a third perspective – a *borderlands* viewpoint – contextualize the history below? According to its proponents, the border itself possesses agency, generating a border culture along the forty-ninth parallel. If Isern and Shepard are correct, then my history that follows offers some support, but only if one accepts Sharp's statement about the Canadian and US transcontinental railways' dividing the continental Plains. If it is true, then the border and the adjacent railway lines produced two hinterlands.[14] The Canadian Pacific Railway (CPR) carried raw materials eastward to the Canadian metropolis along the St Lawrence River, not southward to the United States along, for example, the Whoop-Up Trail. Even when prairie wheat flowed westward to the port of Vancouver, it shipped via the CPR, which earned wealth for the eastern metropolis. Similarly, manufactured goods flowed from east to west, thereby making the prairies dependent on the east.

The same was true in the United States, where the Plains became the hinterland to the US metropolis, centring largely on the eastern seaboard, but also in large cities such as Chicago in the Midwest and San Francisco in the west.[15] The Plains split, Sharp argues, because of the formalized boundary that emerged with the Hudson's Bay Company's ceding of the Northwest Territories to Canada in 1870 and the subsequent completion of two transcontinental rail lines. In my mind, these two factors created parallel meanings for the American and Canadian wests relative to each respective east. By extension, the railway and the boundary similarly helped foster one populist ideology that drove education reform among elite education policy makers, on the one hand, and resistance to it among the people, on the other.

Therein lays the paradox of a borderlands approach to the forty-ninth parallel: in creating the shared experience of two hinterlands, the border produced a transnational cultural affinity and sameness on the Plains and prairies that seemingly could not occur in its absence. In other words, pursuing a borderlands perspective seems to take me full circle, back to the continental perspective with which I began. The "horse and cart" debate as to whether the border itself possessed agency, or if the two transcontinental rail lines produced that agency, appears as an elusive topic, and for this history, not a central concern.

As I hope the title "Border Crossings" implies, the history below is certainly the artefact of a border culture – in this case, a transborder political culture that is both moralistic and populist – that places itself at odds with the eastern metropoles. Because of my emphasis on policy elites, and not on liminal peoples such as First Nations, I certainly lack the postcolonial credentials that Isern and Shepard declare essential to a true borderlands approach. On a positive note, however, I seem to sidestep their criticism of "false-prophet" regional scholars writing in any of the three fields from either side of the international boundary. Canadians, they contend, too often assume a defensive nationalism in their writing, while

Americans tend towards a smug complacency by largely ignoring Canadian interpretations of identical intellectual materials.[16] In my case, it seems only fitting that a Saskatchewanian should pay homage to the influence on him of American writing and thinking, or, to put it differently, the degree to which he personifies both a transfer of culture and a continental perspective on the North American Plains.

A NOTE ON SOURCES

A number of primary source materials contribute a great deal to the manuscript. In K–12 education, I rely heavily on *Annual Reports* to the minister of education for Saskatchewan. Each year, beginning in 1906, inspectors of school divisions prepared detailed reports of local activities for the department. In addition, the principals of normal schools and an increasing number of specialists, in areas such as vocational education and household science, made similar submissions.

These reports I treat within the spirit of what Sol Cohen describes as the "language of discourse," whereby a change in education affects can be marked through changes in the system of language.[17] Between 1905 and 1930, Saskatchewan K–12 educational policy makers were speaking a language of educational reform mirroring that of their US cousins, particularly vis-à-vis the *problem* of rural education on the continental Great Plains. The University of Saskatchewan's Murray Library houses these three types of annual reports in the Government Documents section.

A comprehensive collection of the minutes for meetings of the Board of Trustees, for what is now the Saskatoon Public School Division, exists at its central office in downtown Saskatoon. For the period of this history, the division had two boards, one for elementary schools, the other for collegiates, or high schools. The minutes to which I refer are those from the public elementary system.

The College of Education at the University of Saskatchewan also houses a historic collection of textbooks, which includes most of those the province mandated for K–12 schooling beginning in

1905, in addition to a number of others readily available to the province's teachers. Similarly, the Education Library also contains many of the volumes on the reading list that the Saskatchewan Normal School prepared for teachers pursuing certification. Thus students and teachers alike learned about American reform through US authors.

Finally, the University of Saskatchewan's archives houses the personal and Presidential Papers of Walter C. Murray. While numerous historians have used these to produce general histories of the university and its leader, various readings will often produce a plurality of interpretations. When we look through a continental lens similar to the one that Brison used in his history of American philanthropy in Canadian higher education,[18] the re-description that results may well prove of value among those curious about the role of US foundations in Saskatchewan's system of schooling.

◇◇◇◇◇◇

2

◇◇◇◇◇◇

The Continental Plains
in Historical Perspective

THE COMFORT I ALWAYS FELT, WHILE DRIVING FROM LEXINGTON, Kentucky, to Saskatoon, when I left the east-to-west flow of traffic along Interstate 80 in Iowa to head north to Saskatchewan on Interstate 29, and my discomfort as I left the southward flow of Interstate 29 to head back east on Interstate 80 towards Kentucky, were more than simply emotional responses to traffic on American Interstates. They also involved more than a symbolic demarcation. Walter Prescott Webb identifies the Great Plains as the treelees region that begins in the east roughly between the ninety-fourth and ninety-eighth meridians. The gateway to the American west lies along the ninety-eighth meridian, and intersects Interstate 80 in the area between Davenport, Iowa, on the Mississippi, and Omaha, Nebraska, on the Missouri – where I left the east-to-west traffic and turned north. Both Davenport and Omaha sit on the periphery of Iowa, on my route from Kentucky to Saskatchewan.

Thus Webb's physiographical boundary mirrors my own sentimental divide. As I moved northward along Interstate 29, I truly was in familiar territory, since Saskatchewan is part of a continental Great Plains that stretches south from roughly mid-province all the way to Texas, and beyond. It is easy to judge, simply by looking at a physiographical map, that the land in Saskatchewan is largely identical to land in the American Great Plains, albeit with a slightly

TABLE 2.1

Urban and rural Saskatchewan residents, 1901–1931

Year	Total Population	Urban	Rural	% urban	% rural
1901	91,279	14,266	77,013	16	84
1906	257,763	48,462	209,310	16	84
1911	492,432	131,395	361,037	27	73
1916	647,835	176,162	471,673	27	73
1921	757,510	218,958	538,552	29	71
1931	921,785	290,905	630,880	32	68

Source: Census Canada, www.40.statcan.ca/101/cst01/demo62ihtm <26 July 2008>.

shorter growing season. Assessing the similitude of the people, however, is more difficult, particularly when using census figures from the early twentieth century.

This chapter begins with a brief re-examination of Saskatchewan's demographic data from the period 1905–30. It then chronicles anti-Americanism in English Canada from 1812 to 1905 and concludes that attempts to resist American republican influences in what became Ontario never take hold within Saskatchewan.

SASKATCHEWAN'S PEOPLE, 1905–1937

Saskatchewan, much like the states in the US Great Plains, had a largely rural population from its creation in 1905 well into mid-century. The region's rural residents, according to many educational policy makers, had different needs from their urban counterparts, yet typically experienced urban-like schools and curricula. This discrepancy called for more responsiveness to rural needs. Harold Foght identified such a "rural school problem" as he began research for his *Survey* of Saskatchewan education in 1916. Similarly, the government's decision in 1906 to create the University of Saskatchewan, with a College of Agriculture as its central focus, also reflects the province's rural makeup (see Table 2.1).

TABLE 2.2

Urban and rural Saskatchewan students (numbers), 1906–1931

Year	Total	Rural	Village	Town*	City	High school
1906	31,275	19,230		12,045		1,683
1911	70,567	42,580		27,987		3,849
1916	125,590	74,387	19,518	15,174	16,511	6,903
1921	177,968	102,478	31,344	21,455	22,691	7,442
1926	205,962	122,973	37,179	22,055	23,755	8,942
1931	221,556	130,827	39,743	21,995	28,991	7,956

Source: Saskatchewan, Annual Report of the Department of Education of the Province of Saskatchewan, 1906, 1911, 1916, 1921, 1926, and 1931. *In 1906 and 1911, all non-rural students – village, town, and city – were grouped as "town").

TABLE 2.3

Urban and rural Saskatchewan students (percentages), 1906–1931

Year	% rural	% village	% town	% city
1906	61.5		38.5	
1911	60.3		39.7	
1916	59.2	15.5	12.2	13.1
1921	57.6	17.6	12.0	12.8
1926	59.7	18.1	10.7	11.5
1931	59.0	18.0	9.9	13.1

Source: Foght, Survey, 77.

Tables 2.2 and 2.3 confirm that a large majority of Saskatchewan students throughout the period attended rural schools. Although the annual reports of the province's minister of educaton do not distinguish clearly between rural and village schools, the historiography of Canadian and American education seems to group both types as rural schools. Foght's Survey labels roughly 85 per cent of Saskatchewan's school-age children "rural-minded," which in 1916 included all rural, village, and town schools.[1]

TABLE 2.4
Ethnic origins of Saskatchewan residents (numbers), 1911–1931

Year	British	German	French	Scandi-navian	Russian/Ukrainian	Eastern European	First Nations	Other
1911	251,010	68,628	23,251	33,991	18,413	47,742	11,718	37,649
1916	353,098	77,109	32,066	49,708	33,662	68,536	10,902	22,754
1921	400,416	68,202	42,152	58,382	73,440	65,978	12,914	36,026
1926	416,721	96,498	47,030	63,370	87,682	57,682	13,001	38,754
1931	437,836	129,232	50,700	72,684	98,821	72,783	15,268	44,461

Source: Waiser, *Saskatchewan*, 502.

TABLE 2.5
Ethnic origins of Saskatchewan residents (percentages), 1911–1931

Year	British	German	French	Scandi-navian	Russian/Ukrainian	Eastern European	First Nations	Other
1911	51.0	13.9	4.7	6.9	3.7	9.7	2.4	7.6
1916	54.5	11.9	5.0	7.7	5.2	10.6	1.7	3.5
1921	52.9	9.0	5.6	7.7	9.7	8.7	1.7	4.8
1926	50.8	11.8	5.7	7.7	10.7	7.0	1.6	4.7
1931	47.5	14.0	5.5	7.9	10.7	7.9	1.7	4.8

Source: Waiser, *Saskatchewan*, 502.

Determining the period's rural-to-urban ratio of Saskatchewan's population is a relatively simple process, but the ethnic
makeup is another matter entirely (see Tables 2.4 and 2.5). The
census data tend to call "British" those residents who were born in
the United States or Britons who emigrated from the United States.
As the tables clearly suggest, the census did not treat US-born
residents as an ethnic group unto themselves. Why the government lumped all Americans, Britons, and Canadians together as
"British" is difficult to determine. A closer look confirms that the

TABLE 2.6

Saskatchewan residents born in province, 1911–1931

Year	No. born in province (% of total)	Total population
1911	101,854 (20.7%)	492,432
1921	287,652 (38%)	757,510
1931	442,258 (48%)	921,785

Source: Waiser, Saskatchewan, 503.

province never had an Anglo-Celtic majority. A large percentage of Scandinavians who settled in Saskatchewan earlier spent time in the northern US states so the percentage of American residents is much higher than census data suggest. Table 2.6 identifies the number of native-born residents.

Furthermore, census information from the period does not break data down by ethnic group. For example, Russians in Table 2.4 included Russian Orthodox, Russian Doukhobors, Ruthenians (Ukrainians), and old colony Mennonites, to name but a few categories. While each emigrated from Russia (all but the Russian Orthodox to escape assimilation in Europe), each created cohesive cultural sub-communities in the province. In turn, each community wanted its own school. This was also the case on the American Plains. Ultimately this diversity led to a desire within each ethnic group to establish schools and school divisions to ensure cultural persistence and helps explain why resistance to consolidated rural schools endures in Saskatchewan well beyond its zenith in the US Plains states.

Table 2.7 provides a different breakdown of ethnic data. In 1916, as we saw above, Harold Foght surveyed Saskatchewan but breaks down the census data in a slightly different way. He first numbers residents of British origin, including those who entered this world in Canada or the United States – at 54.5 per cent of the total, as in Table 2.5. When he distinguishes between British and Americans, the proportion of "British" is very different from what most Canadian historians, let alone historians of education,

TABLE 2.7
Ethnic origins of Saskatchewan residents, 1916 (according to Harold Foght)

British	US	Austro-Hungarian	Russian	Scandinavian	German	French	Icelandic	Other
33.75%	28.19%	14.6%	9.52%	5.7%	3.4%	1.5%	0.5%	2.84%
218,644	182,625	94,583	61,674	36,927	22,026	9,718	3,239	18,399

Source: Foght, *Survey*, 13.

assume. The Anglo-Celtic majority, so central to the arguments of education historians such as Tomkins, evaporates like a mirage in the prairie summer heat.

Census data indicate that in 1916 there were 87,901 Saskatchewan residents born in the United States.[2] In 1921, the figure was almost identical, at 87,617.[3] Census information for 1931 identifies 73,008 American-born citizens[4] and 17,826 US-born aliens.[5] By 1931, the percentage of British nationals, if one removes the US born from British totals, again indicates no Anglo-Celtic majority like that in other English-speaking provinces. If one subtracts only American citizens from British totals, again the percentage of British remains closer to 35, or at most, 40 per cent of the total – far from an Anglo-Celtic majority. University of Saskatchewan historian Bill Waiser categorizes the American population in the province in 1906 in the following manner: roughly one third are of Yankee stock, another third are expatriate Canadians who lived in the United States before returning to Saskatchewan, and the final third are Scandinavians who settled first in northern states before moving to Canada. If we apply the same breakdown in 1931 – multiplying 90,000 American-born by 3 – the total number of residents who once lived in the United States is likely between 200,00 and 300,000, thereby reducing still further the percentage of British residents in the province.

Whatever the exact percentage of Saskatchewanians who identified themselves as of British origin, if English-Canadian education, as Tomkins suggests, was to serve an Anglo-Celtic, Protestant, anti-American majority, that majority did not exist in Saskatchewan. Furthermore, including the American born – representing the culture that English-Canadian education was destined to resist – among those who identify themselves as British makes little sense. I here assume that people of British origin in the province between 1905 and 1930 constituted about 35 per cent of the total.

ANTI-AMERICANISM IN ENGLISH CANADA, 1812–1905

At the time of Confederation in 1867, anti-Americanism and fears of US expansion following the Union victory in the Civil War and possible reprisals for Britain's support of the South during the conflict spurred the union of the British North American colonies.[6] There was and is, as Seymour Martin Lipset suggests, no ideology of Canadianism to unite a group of quasi-independent colonies under one identity.[7] There was, however, a common fear. In 1867, anti-Americanism, dependence on Britain, and the need of sizeable minority groups, such as Roman Catholics in Ontario, for support and survival were enough to found a new nation. As Canada expanded westward, however, nation-building and later province-building forced divergent political cultures to develop.

Canada's westernmost province, British Columbia, joined Confederation in 1871 largely in response to eastern fears over potential US expansion – what the Americans called their "manifest destiny" – into the territories between Manitoba and British Columbia, which included what would become Saskatchewan and Alberta in 1905. Prime Minister John A. Macdonald's project of building a transcontinental railway was a further attempt to lay claim to this broad expanse of Canadian prairie.[8] It is safe to say therefore fear of American expansion and influence into Canada's west were widespread in Canada's east from 1867 until 1900 and beyond. The east had long been anxious about US cultural incursion, particularly in education.

Even before the War of 1812, the wide employment of American teachers in Upper Canada (later Ontario) was cause for grave concern among people who loathed republican ideals.[9] As president of the General Board of Education in Upper Canada, Anglican Bishop

John Strachan of Toronto challenged democratic and republican tendencies he saw as infecting the country.[10] Unfriendly foreign (American) teachers were often, he felt, to blame. The rebellions of 1837 in Lower and Upper Canada, many observers believed, served only to confirm the pernicious quality of "revolutionary-minded" American teachers in Upper Canada.

As dangerous as these adventuresome American teachers might seem to the spiritual and intellectual wellness of the British North American subject, even more perilous was the abundance of US school textbooks that confronted Egerton Ryerson during his tenure as superintendent of Schools in Canada West (successor to Upper Canada beginning in 1841). Their use of American textbooks in Canada West (later Ontario), he declared, was both "anti-British and unpatriotic."[11] Such concerns regarding the use of American textbooks led him to promote standardization of textbooks starting with the *Irish Readers*. Though neither English nor Canadian in origin, these pro-imperial volumes were a positive alternative, believed Ryerson, to anything coming from the United States. Developing a standardized list of school textbooks signalled more than a shift in preference away from American publications to those of the British Empire. As Bruce Curtis writes eloquently, "The curricular reforms of 1846 transformed the social identity of the schoolbook by making it an instrument of state policy. Through these reforms school knowledge became state knowledge."[12]

Concerns over American textbooks, or at least what they might represent, antedate Confederation. As one British visitor, Dr Thomas Rolph, observed in 1833: "It is really melancholy to traverse the province and go into many of the common schools; you find a herd of children instructed by some anti-British adventurer instilling in the young ... mind sentiments hostile to the parent state; false accounts of the late war ... geographies setting [American cities] as the largest and finest in the world; historical reading books describing the American population as the most free and enlightened under heaven and American spelling-books, dictionaries and grammar teaching them an anti-British dialect and idiom."[13]

Educational policy in Upper Canada/Canada West sought to resist American influences, while preserving ties with the empire. Opposition to American ideals was ubiquitous in eastern Canada but, I argue below, never took hold in Saskatchewan. Whereas many nineteenth-century English Canadians revered continuity, tradition, and authority,[14] by the early twentieth century in Saskatchewan such traditionalist notions were giving way to a moralistic claim for the public good.

With Manitoba and British Columbia in Confederation, the transcontinental railway complete, and the spectre of American manifest destiny abating, by 1905 Canada's political landscape had changed dramatically.[15] Once free land on the US frontier had gone, a flood of immigrants entered the Canadian prairies. The result was the movement of various aspects of American culture to Saskatchewan.

◇◇◇◇◇◇◇

3

◇◇◇◇◇◇◇

US Culture
in Saskatchewan

TYPICAL STUDIES OF CANADIAN CULTURE AND HISTORY EXAMINE the nation's development from east to west or as a series of movements running parallel to but seldom crossing the US border. What I propose in this chapter is to look at Saskatchewan between 1905 and 1937 in an entirely different way. If we view prairie society and culture along a south–north path from the American Midwest and Plains into Saskatchewan, the picture that emerges is quite distinctive. Indeed, a handful of writers, both American and Canadian, assumed such a perspective in the first half of the twentieth century. They found that the passage of American culture to Saskatchewan resembles a spring breeze emanating from the south, carrying with it a wide variety of cultural flora and fauna, transplanting them to a *virgin soil* ripe for any seed that might flourish there.[1] That the seeds of American culture adapted so easily to the stark physiographical reality of the Canadian prairie is a reflection of the germination of these original seeds in an environment equally isolated, dry, and forbidding as their new garden. Although similar winds blew from Canada's east, the accompanying cultural strains encountered resistant soil and robust, far more fruitful American hybrids. Indeed, for many a Saskatchewan farmer, there was only wind and little else coming from Canada's east.

In describing Saskatchewan as "virgin soil," I do so in two distinct but related ways. In a literal sense, few European or US settlers had broken the province's soil in 1905. Saskatchewan and its neighbouring new province, Alberta, became the "last best west" once free land on the US frontier disappeared. Saskatchewan was on the frontier of Canadian settlement and its economic and social development in 1905. In a figurative sense it was largely devoid of definitive culture, Canadian or otherwise, apart from the scattered First Nations and Métis cultures already there. The province's institutions were certainly British and Canadian, its official language English, and its citizens subject to laws from Ottawa and the new provincial capital in Regina.

Yet the meaning and practice of life in Saskatchewan in 1905 awaited cultural imprint. American culture vied with eastern Canadian and British for influence, and a distinctive northern European cultural strain also helped forge political and economic life early in the twentieth century. Many Scandinavian settlers made their way to Canada's west first through the American Midwest and Plains. This hybrid American–Scandinavian political and economic sensibility left a lasting legacy. This situation contrasted sharply with Ontario's, whose cultural imprint was British from its outset. Loyalist migration from the American states following the Revolutionary War of 1776–83 simply confirmed the British character of the loyalist colony in Upper Canada/Canada West/Ontario. Unlike Ontario and eastern Canada's tendency to resist American culture, Saskatchewan needed and welcomed American cultural influences because of the common challenges of life on the North American Great Plains. Few historians of Canada, and even fewer of Saskatchewan education, have told the story of American stimulus in the province's early years.

When writing of culture, I rely on the theory of William H. Sewell, Jr, who conceives of culture as *meaning* and *practice,* particularly as the process of *language* reflects it. Sewell's notion provides a broad conceptual framework around a very complex term and helps me understand what culture is. For political culture, I invoke Daniel Elazar, who describes the meaning, practice, and language of the *moralistic* political subculture of the US Midwestern and Plains states – the early home of most US immigrants to Saskatchewan and Alberta. I apply these two conceptions of culture – one more general, and the other political – in a complementary manner.

Their findings suggest to me that the meanings of democratic government, of the east and its relationship to the west, and of the land itself were very similar in these neighbouring continental polities. I do not mean to suggest that American culture dominated Saskatchewan's. I do, however, examine the influence of US culture on Saskatchewan, and I challenge standard histories that Canada's west was simply a replica of its east, or that westerners opposed American culture and in effect just combined Ontario and British influences.

For a host of reasons, Saskatchewan welcomed US culture. Prairie agricultural practices copied those to the south, largely because dryland farming originated on the American Great Plains. Canadians reproduced US images of the frontier in their efforts to entice settlers, especially Americans who knew dryland farming techniques and therefore, they believed, could most readily adapt to the harsh realities of the Canadian prairie. Finally, there quickly evolved linguistic similarities among the progressive and populist movements in both nations.

This chapter first looks at mechanisms through which US Midwestern and Plains culture moved northward to Saskatchewan. It then explores how the province received the meanings, practices, and language indicative of a continental Plains culture. A conclusion draws out the implications of this cultural transfer for the setting up and governance of education in the new province.

CULTURAL TRANSFER TO SASKATCHEWAN

Culture is not a static entity, but rather something in the process of constant change. Not surprisingly, cultural ideas and forms transfer from one geographical location to another, which then adapts and redefines them to suit the new location and integrates these into its existing cultural norms. Five notable mechanisms of transfer shaped Saskatchewan's emerging culture: *immigration*: the movement from one nation-state to another of people who take with them their meanings, practice, and language; *organizations and publications*: the introduction of branches of organizations that exist in other locations (e.g., the Grange) and the free flow of publications, including newspapers, academic journals, and professional publications, that disseminate cultural knowledge to receiving societies (e.g., the *Grain Growers Guide*); the *sociological tour*, where individuals travel to other cultures and return with experience, knowledge, and practice; *advanced education* abroad; and *visits by experts* from afar who bring with them the way they do things back home (e.g., Aaron Sapiro's spreading of cooperative forms of production across North America).

The Canadian prairies experienced each mechanism of cultural transfer from the United States in varying degrees. Physiographical similarities between the American Plains and Saskatchewan prairie, and the parallel lived experience that accompanied geographical setting, also led to Saskatchewan's adoption of American culture.[2]

Immigration

The movement of Americans to the Canadian prairies generated extensive documentation. According to University of Saskatchewan historian Bill Waiser, the 1906 census of Canada counted 35,464 "Americans" living in the infant province:[3] one third were native-born US citizens, another third expatriate Canadians, and the remainder northern Europeans who had settled first in the northern American states.[4] US historian Paul Sharp suggests that by 1920 Alberta and Saskatchewan had close to 1.25 million American immigrants.[5] The majority of these settled in the province of Alberta. The newcomers included many from the Midwestern and Plains states of the Dakotas, Iowa, Kansas, Minnesota, Missouri, Montana, and Utah.[6] Saskatchewan provincial historian, John Archer, maintains that the Saskatchewan Valley Land Company alone lured 50,000 American families to a large swath of land bordering on the south and north by the province's two largest cities, Regina and Saskatoon.[7]

Like Sharp, Canadian historian Robert Bruce Shepard admits that estimating the number of people entering Canada west of Winnipeg is difficult, but posits that between 20 and 25 per cent more American immigrants entered the country than the federal government originally chronicled.[8] The vast majority who chose Saskatchewan became homesteaders rather than settling in the few urban settings. In 1921, for example, Shepard argues that 77 per cent of American settlers were rural inhabitants, and in 1931, 73 per cent. The majority of Americans hailed from the Plains and Midwestern states of the Dakotas, Iowa, Michigan, Minnesota, and Wisconsin.[9] Not only were the numbers in Saskatchewan higher than Ottawa reported, but American presence was highest in the countryside.

Timing was crucial. University of Regina geographer Randy Widdis posits that the "closing of the American frontier" pushed transborder movement northward. While the British still out-numbered the Americans in Saskatchewan, there were more US newcomers between 1901 and 1906 than Britons (36.8 per cent of the total versus 26.4 per cent, respectively).[10] This ratio continued into the next decade. After 1905, the momentum of American settlement increased relative to British arrivals and produced a disproportionately large US influence that surpassed that of the Anglo Celts within a generation.

While sheer numbers of US settlers tell one story in the movement of American culture to the Canadian prairie, their states of origin reveal another, equally important tale. The vast majority of those who chose the "last best west" in Saskatchewan and Alberta left from the northern Plains and the Midwestern states – states that maintain what American political scientist Daniel J. Elazar describes as a *moralistic* political culture. This political orientation set them apart from other political subcultures and regions within the United States. To put it another way, those who tended to immigrate to Saskatchewan and Alberta from the United States brought with them very specific ideas as to the meaning and practice of government, the meaning of the east, and the meaning of the west itself.

Elazar's ground-breaking examination divides American political culture into three separate but related subcultures: individualistic, traditionalistic, and moralistic.[11] He believes that while a US national political culture blends all three subcultures, specific regions maintain strong sub-cultures.[12] For those states that comprise the American Midwest and the northern Plains states the dominant political culture is moralistic.[13]

> The moralistic political culture emphasizes the commonwealth conception as the basis for democratic government. Politics, to the moralistic political culture is considered one of the great activities of humanity in its search for the good society – a struggle for power, it is true, but also an effort to exercise power for the betterment of the commonwealth ...

> In the moralistic political culture, individualism is tempered by a general commitment to utilizing communal – preferably non-governmental, but governmental if necessary, power to intervene in to the sphere of private activities when it is considered necessary to do so for the public good or the well-being of the community ...

> Since moralistic political culture rests on the fundamental conception that politics exists primarily as a means for coming to grips with the issues and public concerns of civil society, it also embraces the notion that politics is ideally a matter of concern for every citizen, not just those who are professionally committed to political careers. Indeed, it is the duty of every citizen to participate in the political affairs of his commonwealth ...

> By virtue of its fundamental outlook, the moralistic political culture creates a greater commitment to active government intervention in the economic and social life of the community.[14]

The pioneering American historian of the frontier, Frederick Jackson Turner, complements Elazar's analysis though he speaks in slightly different terms. For Turner, it was the unrelenting challenge of the Great Plains frontier that led settlers away from an individualistic stance towards greater acceptance for, and at times reliance on, government regulation. For the Midwestern pioneer, government intervention became a means of preserving democracy.[15] Both Elazar and Turner's descriptions of moralistic and Great Plains political culture ring true for Saskatchewan.

Furthermore, Widdis cites Canadian historian Arthur Morton in making the case that US settlers who knew dryland farming, more than any other nationality, were responsible for increasing productivity on the Canadian prairies.[16] Widdis also concurs with Elazar as to the state of origin for most of these settlers, suggesting that North Dakota sent the most settlers to the Canadian prairies, with Minnesota a distant second.

New US arrivals, most of them farmers from the Great Plains and Midwest, brought with them a variety of meanings and practices, most notably in agrarian member organizations and political movements, for it was predominantly the American farmer who moved northward into Canada, not the industrialist nor the professional. These organizations were a vital secondary conduit through which Midwestern and American Plains' culture crossed north along longitudinal lines.

Organizations and Publications

Historians of North American agrarian movements agree that much of what developed on the Canadian prairies in the way of protest, reform, and organization in the early twentieth century first took root on the American Plains. The Canadian historian W.L. Morton summarized this relationship in 1950:

> Support of direct legislation was indicative of another element which contributed to the growing political consciousness of the farmers. That was the steady wind of American reformist influence which fanned every flame with precedent, example, and slogan. Not only was there the vivid memory of Populism: not only did the [Grain Growers]Guide carry on its early numbers the old Jacksonian

motto of 'Special privileges for none, and equal rights for all;' not only was direct legislation as popular in the Canadian West during these years as in the north-western American states; there was also the contemporary American Progressive Movement, which reached its climax in the years from 1910 to 1912. Its influence was immediate and insistent on the growth of the reform movement in the Canadian West, and its precept and example, its *vocabulary* and even its name, came to characterize the ferment of political life in the western provinces [emphasis added].[17]

Among the plethora of spreading American organizations, the Grange entered Canada in 1872 and moved west in 1876. Similarly, the American Farmers' Alliance inspired the Farmer's Union of Manitoba shortly thereafter.[18] Because of the affinity between the American Plains and the Canadian prairies, US organizations such as the Farmer's Union, the Non-Partisan League, and the Society of Equity moved northward with the settlers.[19]

The transfer of Midwestern and Plains political culture, agrarian organizations, and protest movements was greatly facilitated by the influence of Canadian print publications, most notably the *Grain Grower's Guide,* the *Nutcracker,* and the *Western Producer,* and also the US *Leader.* Sharp posits that the *Guide* and the *Leader* were similar in both content and style: each performed an educational function, identified a moral to the reader, and preached a gospel invoking revolt in the wheat belt.[20] The *Western Producer,* printed in Saskatoon from the early 1920s until today, was first *Turner's Weekly* and became the *Progressive* in 1923. In its early stages, the paper's motto was "Reliable News, Unfettered Opinions, and Western Rights."

Western Canadian publications' coverage of US activities further spread culture northward. For example, Canadian Non-partisan League newspapers followed the successes of the North Dakota League very closely, often publishing articles by North Dakota legislator C.W. McDonnell in papers such as the *Grain Grower's Guide.*[21] Furthermore, publications in both countries assumed similar languages of protest and insult, including phrases such as "Big Biz" for industry and, the "Kept Press" for opposing journals, to name just two. Cartoons were a popular source of criticism and ridicule on both sides of the border. Canadian writers often simply substituted the Canadian Manufacturers' Association for the American Manufacturers' Association,[22] so similar was the experience of the Canadian farmer relative to that of his American cousin.

Western Canadian farmers learned about American practice, agrarian politics, and revolt through a variety of media. In addition to reading and hearing about activities south of the forty-ninth parallel, the "sociological tour" became a common means for Saskatchewanians to borrow from their neighbours to the south. Individuals and groups toured the American Midwest and Plains states frequently, and American experts responded in kind to spread the gospel of reform. American popular culture also made its way to Saskatchewan.

The Sociological Tour[23]

Existing literature says little about organized sojourns from the Canadian prairies to the United States. Governments supported fact-finding missions southward. For example, in 1900 in the midst of a debate over grain elevators and shipping, a federal commission dispatched two members to Minnesota to assess the storage and shipment of grain there.[24] Their inquiry led to the Manitoba Grain Act, which shaped Saskatchewan's later legislation.

The 1916 election campaign for North Dakota's state legislature lured a few Saskatchewanians south to gain experience with formation and fomentation of third parties. Among the visitors was a farmer from outside Swift Current, in the southwest of the province. S.E. Haight worked in the campaign for North Dakota's Non Partisan League (NPL) and on his return home in July 1916 organized a similar league.[25] These efforts, along with many others, brought the NPL's success in North Dakota to the Canadian prairies.

Less formal interactions occurred for a variety of reasons, most notably involving the purchase of American farm machinery. Despite the protests of the Canadian Manufacturers' Association, centred in Ontario – a group that western farmers distrusted – prairie farmers preferred US machinery.[26] Not only did they consider it superior, it usually cost less. One powerful example involved binders. According to Sterling Evans, the tens of thousands of American farmers who emigrated northward between 1900 and 1920 brought their farm implements with them. They, along with European immigrants who settled first in the United States, came to depend on the US product. Roughly 40,000 members of the Order of the Patrons of Industry petitioned Ottawa to reduce the tariff on this and other such implements.[27] Saskatchewan farmers made frequent trips to purchase machinery in the US market, where they learned about widespread opposition there to the American Manufacturer's Association. As a result, farmers on both sides of the boundary shared mistrust for corporations "back east."

Similarly, Saskatchewan farmers frequently exhibited and participated in farm expositions, such as the International Soil Products Exposition in Kansas City, Missouri, in 1918.[28] Such events proliferated across North America and were ideal sites for cultural exchange. Seager Wheeler farmed 40 miles north of Saskatoon, competed each year at several US expositions, and became world Wheat King five times.[29] Indeed, flipping through the pages of the *Grain Growers Guide* and *Western Producer*, one learns quickly that the *Guide* is emblematic of the continental nature of an agrarian economy and culture. It weekly reported commodity prices from a variety of economic centres, including Winnipeg, Chicago, and St Paul, Minnesota. Many factors linked the Canadian and US agricultural communities inextricably. What happened in one necessarily influenced the other.

For example, at a time when the internal combustion engine was in its infancy on the farm, and draft horses were the major source of "horse power," horse-pulling contests were another site of cultural transfer. US teams of horses often headed north to compete in Saskatchewan, and vice versa. Professor E.V. Collins at Iowa State College developed the standard for measuring the amount of weight a team was pulling with his invention of the "dynamometer." Once Saskatchewan had copied it (see Figure 3.1),

Fig. 3.1 The University of Saskatchewan's version of the "dynamometer" (photo after 1924),
first created at Iowa State College in Ames. University of Saskatchewan Archives, A3352.

teams from the province soon challenged several world records, thereby increasing the frequency of contact and the intensity of the rivalry with their American cousins.[30]

To this point, I have emphasized the role of agrarian movements, associations, and industries in cultural transfer. Although agriculture was the key conduit, sociological tours led to cultural borrowings in other sectors. In K–12 education, for example, it was customary for Saskatchewan educators to attend annual meetings of the National Education Association (NEA) in the United States. In 1918, Mr A. Kennedy, inspector of schools for Weyburn, a small town in southeastern Saskatchewan, told the NEA gathering: "Mr. President – the Department of Education of the Government of the Province of Saskatchewan fully appreciates the value of the National Education Association and has requested me to carry to you a message of greeting and good-will. Problems that present themselves to you for your consideration and solution also present themselves to us; and your discussion and solutions are of very great benefit to us."[31]

In higher education, in 1907 the nascent University of Saskatchewan's president, Walter Murray, and several members of its board of governors visited many of the Midwest's large land-grant universities and private institutions, including the University of Wisconsin in Madison, Washington University in St Louis, and a variety of agricultural research stations. Their experience resulted in a template for their university that was unlike any other in Canada.[32]

American popular culture travelled north as well. For example, Midwest baseball teams frequented Saskatchewan communities in summer, particularly those with African-American players, whose nation banned them from play.[33] By the 1920s, baseball was the province's second-most popular sport, after hockey. Similarly, radio listeners could easily pick up American broadcasts from cities such as Denver and Chicago.[34] Chautauqua also arrived in the 1920s, making what Theodore ('Teddy') Roosevelt (US president 1901–09) called "the most American thing in America" a staple on the Canadian prairies.[35] American popular culture permeated the province of Saskatchewan.

Not all that the region borrowed from the United States, however, was positive. The Saskatchewan chapter of the Ku Klux Klan found fertile soil in a province where some residents felt anxious about what they saw as Catholic and central/eastern European infiltration into a society that many of them perceived as Protestant and British; by 1929, the chapter boasted 25,000 members.[36] Such an episode is a revealing example of how the Canadian prairies adapted American culture to its own purposes. Reinventing the Klan as a pro-British and Protestant organization, adherents played on similar nativist sentiments, calling for an exclusionist immigration policy and the removal of public funding for Catholic and/or francophone schools. While their activities never reached the level of violence of their American counterparts, the ritualistic burning of crosses was not an uncommon site. The Ku Klux Klan also exercised varying levels of influence among all the major political parties throughout the late 1920s and into the 1930s.[37]

Higher Education Abroad

Because of the rural, agrarian makeup of Saskatchewan between 1905 and 1937, few residents went to study in the United States. In 1907, the province set up a university in Saskatoon, which expanded only gradually, suggesting that higher education was not a priority for most people. The "culture of aspiration" that existed in the United States did not begin to develop in Saskatchewan until after the First World War ended in 1918. Yet the provincial university, from its outset, hired some faculty members who had been born in or studied in the United States. According to university historian Arthur S. Morton, two of its first five instructors had American training. In 1910, when it hired five more profesors, three had postgraduate degrees from Ivy League universities. In 1911, one of two new hires was from the United States; in 1913, two of three.[38] Although Saskatchewanians were not generally pursuing higher education in the United States, higher education in the province was certainly affected by American institutions for higher learning.[39]

In the 1920s, however, a few K–12 teachers headed south for studies. Following Harold Foght's 1918 *Survey* of the province's schools, several educationists working for the provincial Department of Education, and a handful of teachers, began advanced studies in a variety of fields, all at two campuses: the University of Chicago or New York's Columbia University – the bastions of Progressive education reform in the United States. For example, in 1927, Miss L.P. Lewis, a teacher in the Saskatoon School District, received 18 months' leave to complete her primary work at Columbia University.[40] In the decade of the 1920s, about 10 other educational elites pursued similar opportunities. The principal of the Regina Normal School and a mathematics instructor at the Saskatoon Normal School completed PhDs in education psychology at Columbia's Teacher's College and in mathematics at Chicago, respectively.[41] Therefore, while American higher education remained beyond the means of most people in Saskatchewan occasionally American higher education came to the people.

In a similar fashion, the American expert travelled northward to extend innovation to the people of the province.

The American Expert[42]

When Saskatchewan's policy makers sought inspiration for their uniquely prairie travails, often they looked south for their guidance, rather than east. One prominent example of this receptivity to American models is the messianic work of Aaron Sapiro of California, whose commitment to cooperative forms of production attracted large audiences in the province on several occasions, and helped lay the foundation for the Saskatchewan Wheat Pool – a producers' cooperative that continues today. Another is the government's decision in 1916 to hire Harold Foght, an expert on rural education from the US Bureau of Education in Washington, DC, to survey the province's K–12 system of education.

The advent of the expert was certainly not indigenous to North America, but instead was an outgrowth of a North Atlantic policy community that sought scientific and rational solutions to political and social problems. Former University of Saskatchewan political scientist David Laycock argues: "Technocracy in this broad sense is the first principle of social engineering in the tradition of Anglo-American utilitarianism, and has been of great importance in the approaches that western political elites have taken to the problems of policy determination and administration over the last century."[43] Prairie Canadian populism developed within this context – what US commentators call "social efficiency" – with both populists and technocrats absorbing into their ideology aspects of the other, seemingly antithetical components. This development encouraged social-democratic populists in Saskatchewan, for example, to push for anti-statist local control by the people, while still abiding the expert influence of people such as Aaron Sapiro, who articulated a centralized, technocratic planning of cooperative grain production and marketing.[44] Balancing local and centralized control was a constant challenge for both governments and cooperatives in Saskatchewan between 1910 and 1945.

Although scientific management, technocracy, and social efficiency were not American inventions, when looking for policy solutions to prairie Canadian problems, Saskatchewan's policy makers and local patrons alike turned to American proponents' adaptations of these ideologies for inspiration. This was as true in the field of agriculture as it was in education.

The advent of producer cooperatives was far from an American idea. Nevertheless, that the grain growers of Saskatchewan should turn to a lawyer from California to educate farmers about the benefits of pooling wheat is testimony to their faith in American methods. Sapiro's maxim "Get wise! Organize!" became the rallying cry for a generation of Saskatchewan farmers who listened to his message in Saskatoon in the summer of 1923. One of those who heard his speech in Saskatoon was the University of Saskatchewan historian Frank Underhill. Fifty years later, he wrote: "His speech was the most magnificent to which I have ever listened."[45] Throughout 1923 and 1924, the *Western Producer* carried almost-weekly articles on Sapiro, reproducing his speeches from locales across the prairie provinces at a time when enthusiasm for and commitment to a unified approach to pooling and marketing wheat among farmers was weakening. It was Sapiro's passion and wisdom, which he gained organizing California fruit producers, that led farming leaders in Saskatchewan to seek his guidance and counsel.

In the spring of 1923, some northern US states, particularly Minnesota, had similarly recruited Sapiro and others to jump start their own efforts at establishing producer cooperatives. As he was to do in Saskatchewan a few months later, Sapiro praised the cooperative spirit of Minnesota farmers while criticizing their decision to pursue a producer's cooperative plan along the lines of the Rochdale consumer cooperative established in England in 1844.[46] While not all aspects of the Sapiro Plan took shape in the state of Minnesota, his agitation for a different approach to cooperative endeavours had a lasting impact across the North

American continent.[47] Most significant, however, Saskatchewan cooperative organizers used the same method of agitation employed by their Minnesotan cousins.

Other features of American agricultural practice came northward in addition to the expert. Shepard credits much of the rural landscape that humans developed on the Canadian prairies to American antecedents. For example, the "vernacular architecture" of the American homestead became the norm in Saskatchewan, with its penchant for straight furrows and fence lines; considered "correct" because they were straight. The farmhouse, barn, and schoolhouse also bore the US-style look and architecture.[48] Shepard also credits the network of grain elevators – those most obvious of prairie landmarks –to the work of the American railway magnate William C. Van Horne.[49] Though born in the United States, Van Horne became president of the Canadian Pacific Railway and played a key role in laying the CPR through Saskatchewan.

In regard to Foght's *Survey* of 1918, the decision to recruit an American expert on rural education was not only a tacit acceptance of American educational forms and functions, but also an implicit rejection of models from Canada's east. The school survey movement itself was very much an American creation, starting in 1911 with Paul Hanus, a Harvard professor in the history and art of teaching.[50] That Saskatchewan's Department of Education would choose an American expert, and not a Canadian, suggests that rural education in the province was undergoing growing pains similar to those in US rural areas. Several August issues of *Turner's Weekly* in 1919 contained lengthy articles on the "Rural Education Problem" in Saskatchewan.[51] The consolidation movement, which sought to combine independent schools and districts into larger, centralized, and more efficient entities, had begun in American urban school divisions in the nineteenth century and was already in full swing among US rural school divisions by the end of the First World War. This effort, states David Tyack, marked an ongoing struggle between local or community control and professionalism.[52] Like many of their US counterparts, Saskatchewan experts were knocking at the doors of rural schools, expecting everyone to welcome their influence. Not everybody did.

The Foght *Survey* of 1918 reveals the influence of American models of education in terms of both form and content. I discuss the report's content below in later chapters. In form, however, the decision to hire an expert from Washington, DC, is itself a telling example of Saskatchewan policy makers' keenness to replicate American processes on the Canadian plains. That Saskatchewan education policy makers anticipated Foght's recommendation for wholesale consolidation long before his survey began seems certain, given that in 1917 the province had about four thousand,school divisions, many with only one school, and that for years prior to the *Survey* Saskatchewan school inspectors had consistently urged large-scale consolidation. Saskatchewan policy makers had already learned a valuable lesson from their American counterparts – that employing an expert, especially from the US Bureau of Education, was an effective means to legitimate pre-existing decisions. David Tyack confirms: "But as the [school survey] movement matured, it became increasingly a device for 'Progressive' superintendents to enlist the aid of outsiders to make changes they wanted anyway ... Supporting the survey movement was a network of university professors, administrative progressives in the city school systems, the U.S. Bureau of Education, lay reformers in civic organizations, and foundations."[53] Whether in the field of agriculture policy or education policy, Saskatchewan legislators had adopted the American practice of relying on the expert to inform policy decisions – a hallmark of the American Progressive movement.[54]

American Culture on the Prairies: Meaning, Practice, and Language

To this point I have accounted for the manner in which American culture, particularly the moralistic political culture of the Midwestern and northern Plains states, moved northward into Saskatchewan. My task now is to verify that what William H. Sewell, Jr, defines as the critical attributes of culture – meaning, practice, and language – were in fact received by the residents of the province. In so doing, I focus on the meanings, practice, and language of what I consider the three crucial constructs of American culture that ultimately influenced Saskatchewan policy making: first, conceptions of democratic government, since these are direct reflections of political culture, with schools themselves being intensely democratic political entities; second, the concept of the east and its powerful "nabobs" – that locus which Saskatchewan policy makers sought to resist, leading them instead to turn southward for their inspiration (the language of agrarian protest on the prairies linked democracy and the east inextricably, as opposites); and, third, the concept of the west, which includes the land itself.

Ultimately – as a brief conclusion intimates – the multi-faceted elements of cultural transfer and the resulting understandings of democracy, the east, and the west came together to shape life and rural schools on the western Canadian frontier. The meaning, practice, and language of US Midwestern and northern Plains culture will replicate themselves on the Canadian prairies, albeit with a time lag of roughly 15–20 years after inception.

Democratic Government

Explicit within Saskatchewan's political culture beginning in 1905 is a concept of democratic government that is both moralistic and social democratic. Implicit within it is a voice of protest against what seemed an asymmetric economic and political relationship with the prairie region and Canada's east. This asymmetry was obvious across the American Great Plains prior to 1905. David Laycock suggests that Canada's "prairie citizens often viewed the electoral practices of the southern republic – first male and then universal suffrage, experimentation with instruments of direct democracy, the primaries, and open conventions for leadership selection – as superior to those of their own reluctantly democratic polity."[55] They often gazed south, rather than east, for their political meaning and inspiration.

American *moralistic* political subculture was obvious in prairie populism in this era. Within the *social-democratic* strain of prairie populism, which dominated Saskatchewan, democracy required "a more egalitarian, state-enforced, and co-ordinated distribution of goods and opportunities, flowing from extensive citizen participation in social institutions."[56] This branch of populism expected government involvement in the lives of citizens.[57]

Radical-democratic populism emanated from the rural US west, says Laycock, and tended to reject party politics in favour of maintaining a fervent belief in participatory democracy and group government.[58] Crypto-liberal populism was the most influential form of protest on the prairies in the 1910s and 1920s, favouring the language of direct democracy, referendum, and recall as a means for the people to retain political power over the parties.[59] Such ideas drew heavily from American populist and Progressive movements.

Paul Sharp observes:

The western Canadian farmer who protested against a high tariff, trusts and combines, and "money power" in 1911 did so in the best Jeffersonian tradition. His protests were rooted in the same soil of Lockean thought and evangelical Protestantism and sprang from the same grievances that had produced the Grange, the Farmers' Alliance, and Populism in the United States. His crusade coincided with and sought the same fundamental objectives as the Farmers' Union, the Society of Equity, Robert M. LaFollette's "Progressivism," and Woodrow Wilson's "New Freedom." This was no accident. The impact of monopolistic consolidation of Canadian industry hit the prairie farmer with such force during these years that in self-defence he turned to reforms similar to those advocated by American muckrakers and reformers in their "quest for social justice."[60]

These shared experiences among prairie social democrats and moralistic plainsmen found their greatest expression in the practice of political protest.

The *practice* of democratic government on the Canadian prairies responded, of course, to the parliamentary structures of Westminster's British North America Act of 1867 and Ottawa's Saskatchewan Act of 1905. Regardless, Saskatchewanians adapted populist and Progressive democratic ideals to the Canadian milieu. Among these was the practice of forming third parties to protest and resist the power and influence of the two-party structure. In the 1920s, the Canadian Progressive Party, an outgrowth of the Non-Partisan League (NPL), challenged the existing two-party structure, which inevitably favoured the more populous central provinces of Ontario and Quebec.[61] The politics of protest was more successful at the national level in Canada than in the United States, albeit fleetingly: the Progressives won a majority of western seats in the 1921 federal election and maintained the balance of power in the House of Commons, under a Liberal minority government, until the election of 1925.[62]

At the provincial level, third parties found their greatest success in Alberta and Saskatchewan, at first in rural areas. The Cooperative Commonwealth Federation (CCF) increased its support within Saskatchewan throughout the 1930s and formed the government in 1944. The CCF, now the New Democratic Party (NDP), has dominated provincial politics in the province ever since. In Alberta, the Social Credit Party dominated in a similar way into the 1970s, when the Conservatives began a long period of rule, which continues to this day. While the west persisted as one locus for third-party formation in Canada, these parties never wielded influence beyond the regions in which they were born and, as a result, their influence at the national level remains limited (recent NDP success in Ottawa notwithstanding).

Even though political protests in Canada took their inspiration from their southern kin, third parties there had little success at the state level among northern US states. The notable exception was the NPL's victory in North Dakota's state legislature in 1916. Success there soon spread north through the efforts of a few Saskatchewanians who worked for the NPL in the North Dakota campaign.[63] At the federal level, Progressivism remained largely contained within the existing structure of the Democratic and

Republican parties. (Republican Theodore Roosevelt ran as a Progressive for a third term as president in 1912, taking 27.4 per cent of the popular vote.)[64] The most hopeful attempt at thrusting the Progressive movement onto the national stage occurred with Republican Senator Robert LaFollette of Wisconsin's campaign for the Presidency in 1924 – an attempt that garnered 16.6 per cent of the popular vote, finishing second behind victor Calvin Coolidge; after LaFollette's defeat the Progressive party disbanded.[65] Though impressive, this would be the final occasion when a Progressive-inspired program would enter the American national arena. Such results, however, show that protest politics first gained prominence on the American Plains before migrating northward. Closely related to these political protests were objections to the centripetal concentration of economic power in the east.

The "Down-East Nabobs"

On both the Canadian prairies and the American plains, eastern corporations, or trusts, were the focal points of popular, grass-roots revolt and protest. Given that these "easts" represented the geographical centre of economic disparity, monopoly, and exploitation in both nations, it is little wonder that many people in Saskatchewan would resist these influences in a manner similar to their American cousins. The "down-east nabobs" of Bay Street (the financial core of Toronto) as many western farmers scurrilously identified the corporate heads there, and their corporations, represented what the west was to progress away from, and not toward. The meaning of the east relative to the west was shared across the continental Great Plains.

Richard Hofstadter's *Age of Reform* articulates the conspiratorial mentality maintained by agrarian populists. American populists believed that "the interests" intentionally oppressed farmers and workers alike. As populism and Progressivism merged after 1900, at the beginning of the twentieth century these interests took on the moniker of the "plutocracy." The plutocrats were represented by the newly rich, or people who gained their fortunes through corruption or graft, or more generally as

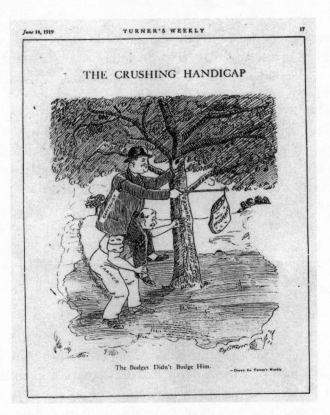

THE CRUSHING HANDICAP

The Budget Didn't Budge Him.

— Drawn for Turner's Weekly

Fig. 3.2 "The Crushing Handicap" (1919). A common theme in many western Canadian periodicals
of the period: national prosperity created on the back of the western farmer.
Turner's Weekly, 14 June 1919, reprinted with the permission of the *Western Producer*.

the "masters of the great corporation."[66] The heads of railway corporations, who grew wealthy on the backs of underpaid workers
while charging excessive fees on western farmers, were the most
obvious of plutocrats, in addition to the American Manufacturers'
Association, which provided an organizational target for western
protest. Although plutocrats existed in many communities, protest movements associated them most with eastern corporate
interests and the likes of fabulously wealthy businessmen such
as Andrew Carnegie, J. Pierpont Morgan, and John D. Rockefeller,
Sr and Jr.[67]

The trust-busting activities that prevailed south of the border
under the leadership of Teddy Roosevelt in the first decade of the

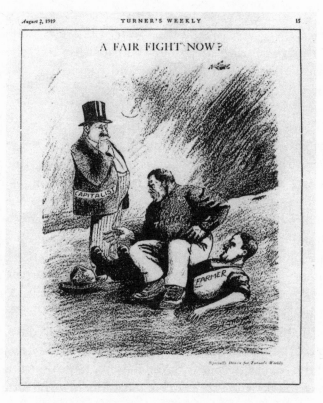

Fig. 3.3 "A Fair Fight Now?" (1919) shows the prairie farmer under the burden of
Ottawa's tariff, which favoured the eastern capitalist. *Turner's Weekly*, 2 August 1919,
reprinted with the permission of the *Western Producer*.

twentieth century assumed a less aggressive and ambitious form
in western Canada some 10–20 years later. Nevertheless, prairie
farmers particularly resented the activities of corporations such
as the Canadian Pacific Railway, the Canadian National Railways,
and the Canadian Manufacturers' Association, all with headquar-
ters centred in the east. Laycock suggests that all branches of
prairie populism saw the plutocracy as opposing the people, and
that social-democratic circles associated party politics with corporate control.[68] For many prairie farmers, the east represented
industry, tariffs, and protectionism. In political terms, it epitomized domination of the west by the Liberal and Conservative parties. Political cartoons appeared frequently in farmer's periodicals

such as *Turner's Weekly* and the *Western Producer* and captured the relationship between farmer and capitalist and, correspondingly, west and east (see Figures 3.2 and 3.3).

The "Last Best West"

One can think of Canada's west in at least two distinct ways. The first, the physiographical west, encapsulates the practice of farming and the living of rural life on the frontier or Great Plains. The second includes the constructed west, or the manner in which the federal government represented and advertised the west and the meaning it contained for the settlers. Although most Canadian historians distinguish American and Canadian wests, particularly along political lines, for many settlers the Canadian west was an extension of the American west, both physiographically and in its meaning (see Figures 3.4 and 3.5).

For many Europeans, Canada, like the United States, came to symbolize the existence of free land – 160 acres of it. Canada at the turn of the twentieth century offered immigrants the same amount of land as the US Homestead Act of 1862. American historians of the frontier, including Frederick Jackson Turner and Walter Prescott Webb, make virtually no distinction between the American and Canadian wests, whether one views each as a frontier or as part of the continental Great Plains.[69] For Turner, the frontier is the frontier, whether in the Canadian, Australian, or American context. The existence of inexpensive, expansive tracts of land marks the edge of the frontier (see Figure 3.6). The only difference between the American frontier and its Canadian equivalent is the timing of settlement, with Canada's following the end of its southern counterpart's by some twenty years, if we follow Turner's reported "end" to the American frontier. For the American historian Richard Slotkin, Turner simply substituted a geographical entity (the west) for a class-based entity (agrarian/industrialist) as the dividing discipline in American history.[70]

For Webb, the ninety-eighth meridian marks the beginning of the Great Plains on the North American continent. He argues that a move from the eastern timberland into the Great Plains

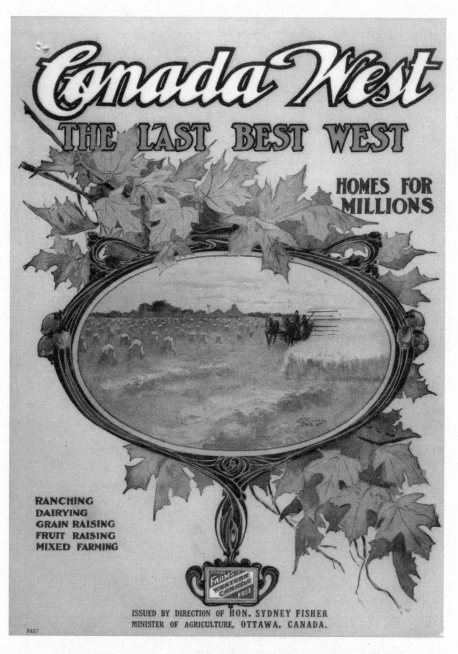

Fig. 3.4 "Canada West: The Last Best West." Federal Ministry of Interior poster 1905–11 implicitly identifies the Canadian prairies as an extension of the American west. Library and Archives Canada, C-030620.

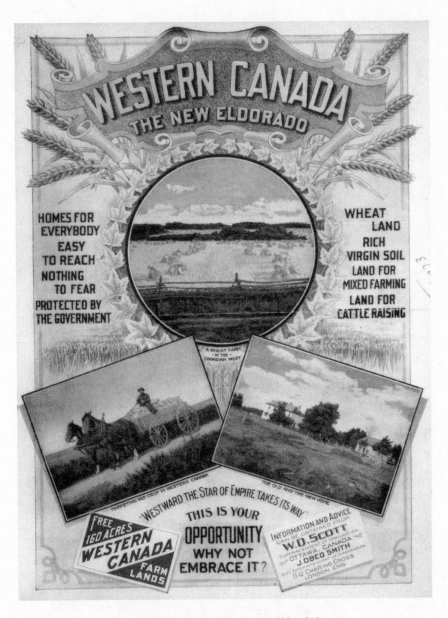

Fig.3.5 "Western Canada: The New Eldorado."
The federal Department of Immigration further characterizes the region as an extension
of the US west. Library and Archives Canada/Department of Employment
and Immigration fonds/C-085854.

Fig. 3.6. "Canada: 160 Acres fritt land" (Canada: 160 Acres of Free Land).
Swedish version of a Canadian government advertisement.
Library and Archives Canada, C-132141.

produces an inalterable change in the practice of life: "At this fault [at the ninety-eighth meridian] the ways of life and of living changed. Practically every institution that was carried across it was either broken and remade or else greatly altered. The ways of travel, the weapons, the method of tilling the soil, the plows and other agricultural implements, and even the laws themselves were modified. When people first crossed this line they did not immediately realize the imperceptible change that had taken place in their environment, nor, more is the tragedy, did they foresee the full consequences which that change was to bring in their own characters and in their modes of life."[71]

For Seymour Martin Lipset, it was life in the "grain belt" that produced similar experiences on both sides of the artificial border. "It is highly significant that the first electorally successful social-ist party [the CCF] in the United States or Canada should have developed in the same Great Plains wheat belt that earlier pro-duced the Greenbackers, the Populists, the Non-Partisans, and other agrarian upheaval."[72] In seeing the forty-ninth parallel west of Lake Superior as a man-made, artificial, and arbitrary creation, Sharp goes the furthest in acknowledging that the prairie west and the American Midwest are part of the same environment.

One recent history of the American west complements Sharp and his contemporaries. Richard White posits that US westward migrations tended to follow latitudinal lines. The livestock that travelled with the migrants and the seeds that had grown in the previous, easterly environment adapted most readily to simi-lar climatic conditions along the same parallel. An appeal to the familiar also influenced such migrations. These latitudinal move-ments, however, ceased at the ninety-eighth meridian, that same signpost identified by Webb. There, suggests White, latitudinal influences weakened. "The major geographical marker on the Great Plains was longitude, not latitude; west of the 98th merid-ian the land grew increasingly arid. The advantages offered by migration along a line of latitude dwindled, while the challenge of adjusting to the arid West became preeminent."[73] To put it another way, the west in both countries began beyond this signpost.

When I contemplate the meaning of the prairie west, I feel

myself making history rather than reporting it. It is at this point that I begin to feel viscerally the ongoing debate within the profession about the historian's role – to report history "objectively" or to create it? In keeping with the spirit of this manuscript, I admit freely that what follows is my interpretation of the meaning of the Canadian prairies, albeit with the assistance of American historians, some writing in the *pastoral* tradition. Canadian historians, for very good reasons (or at least they must have seemed so at the time), have created their west in opposition to the American one as a means of both assuming an air of cultural and moral superiority and defining what it means to be Canadian. As one recent commentator has concluded, however, being Canadian often means being *not* American.[74]

Delving into the meaning of the west at the turn of the twentieth century poses a variety of methodological problems. In making such an attempt, I wish to engage meaning through the use of *symbols* as they emerged at that time. William H. Sewell, Jr, in his examination of working-class revolt in France during the French Revolution, aids me in this process:

> Although we [historians] obviously cannot hope to experience what nineteenth century workers experienced or to think their thoughts as they thought them, we can, with a little ingenuity, search out in the surviving records the symbolic forms through which they experienced their world. In part this means constructing the meanings of the words, metaphors, and rhetorical conventions that they used to talk about and think about their experiences ... If we can discover the symbolic content and conceptual coherence of all kinds of working-class experiences, then the worker's adoption of explicit political ideologies will no longer appear as a sudden intrusion of 'ideas' from the outside but as the introduction or elaboration of yet another symbolic framework into lives that – like all ours – were already animated by conceptual issues and problems.[75]

At the beginning of the twenty-first century, a range of factors can explain how and why Canadians may differ from Americans.

At the turn of the twentieth, however, my reading of a variety of texts leads me to conclude that the people who settled Saskatchewan did not worry much about cultural differences between settling in Saskatchewan or, for example, North Dakota, if such differences existed at all. For a large portion of newcomers to the west, it was irrelevant whether they lived under the Stars and Stripes or the Union Jack. The west, either on the American or Canadian prairies, meant largely the same thing: a progression away from more traditional modes of life in the east; opportunities for family prosperity through ownership of land; and in the case of European settlers, a chance to re-create a fragment of Old World society through the collective benefits of homogeneous group settlement and combining that precious heritage with New World freedoms and prosperity.

American writers, particularly historians within the pastoral literary tradition, suggest that western migration has always enticed humankind from the advent of civilization, beginning in the classical age with Virgil's *Aeneid* about the Trojan going to Italy. Henry Nash Smith attributes this same approach to American authors such as William Gilpin, who suggests that each westward thrust of American society produced development superior to its easterly predecessor.[76] What Smith describes as this general law of progress, "so flattering to the West, becomes a guiding command to the American people in moments of decision."[77] As the United States spread westward, so too would the conception of the west as ideal simplicity, virtue, and contentment.[78]

Leo Marx extends Smith's pastoral notions, equating them with the idealization of rural life. Marx's history of westward movement presents agricultural life as morally, aesthetically, and metaphysically superior to urban life in the east.[79] Movement westward headed towards both a simpler and a more complete way of life, but also away from what the poet Walt Whitman described as the "shadow of Europe" and its many conventions. Whitman tied the concept of manifest destiny inexplicably to westerly migration.

John Gast's famous 1872 painting *American Progress* (Figure 3.7) crystallizes the essence of progress through western settlement.

Fig. 3.7 John Gast's *American Progress* (1872). Note railways on the right.
Autry National Center, Los Angeles, 92:126.1.

Art historian Brian W. Dippie comments that its tranquil procession of Civilization leaves behind a bustling city in the east, while
before it lies the panic of the old order, shrouded in darkness.[80]
The image of Civilization, a female form of great beauty, virgin-
like, floating above the plains, is a moving and memorable image of
progress. Railways move from east to west to the right of the painting. Not surprising, these same images reappear on the Canadian
prairies some three decades later.

Knowingly or not, the Canadian government adopted American
symbols of the west: progress, the railway, and prosperity – for its
own program of settlement there. Its massive effort at the turn of
the twentieth century was its second great attempt to lure people
to the prairies – the first, which started in 1885, had failed for a
variety of reasons.[81] Regardless, the United States was far more
successful at gaining settlement onto the Great Plains, and one
cannot help but wonder if American success attracted Canadian
borrowers a generation later.

Fig. 3.8 "Canada West" (1923). The federal Ministry of Immigration and Colonization was seeking settlers from the United Kingdom to ensure the nation's British character. Library and Archives Canada, e000007930.

Fig. 3.9 "Prosperity Follows Settlement in Western Canada" (1921–23).
Cover of a pamphlet for a campaign to attract US immigrants by evoking a
symbol of the west for both countries. University of Saskatchewan, University
Library, Special Collections, Shortt Collection FC3205.2. C21P76 1905.

Fig. 3.10 "Saskatoon[,] Saskatchewan: The Wonder City" (1911). Leaflet cover: the image
of the woman is more modern, but trains still symbolize progress and development.
University of Saskatchewan, University Library, Special Collections,
Canadiana Pamphlet Collection XLIX-166.

Although the flag that accompanies the advent of Canadian
civilization is different (Figure 3.8), the beautiful image of progress
remains largely identical: virgin-like in appearance, bringing bounty
and progress to the west while leaving the Old World behind in the
east. Similarly, the railway, barely visible at the feet of a largely identical female in Figure 3.9, was another constant symbol of progress
and westward settlement on both frontiers.[82] In the early decades
of the twentieth century, Ottawa used many means to attract settlement into the Canadian prairies. Minister of the Interior Frank
Oliver (serving 1905–11 in Wilfrid Laurier's Liberal government in
Ottawa) sought more Britons to help keep the nation British. In
so doing, however, he appropriated the railway as the symbol of
progress and civilization that US efforts applied so effectively.

A third symbol of the west in both nations simply identified
the region with prosperity. Figure 3.10 describes the growing city

of Saskatoon as a "wonder city." Canadian historian Gerald Friesen chronicles a variety of interpretive accounts to explain why immigrants sought a new life in the Canadian west. Early Canadian histories of western settlement, he argues, tended to acknowledge the dominant role of Clifford Sifton, Laurier's first minister of the interior (1896–1905). More recent scholarship focuses on the "push and pull" motives of settlers. Not only did the west pull immigrants to Canada through the promise of free land, but the Old World itself, with its lack of social mobility and economic prosperity, pushed many.[83] The two factors combined to produce a meaning of a prosperous west for tens of thousands of Europeans.

CONCLUSION

In addition to perhaps pursuing notions of progress and prosperity, a movement to either the Canadian or the American west gave immigrants the opportunity to re-create a fragment of the Old World community in the New World. Through immigration and settlement practices such as *colony* settlement, whereby a sizeable portion of a European community or kinship group settled in a specific area, large segments of communities could remain largely intact. Patchwork settlements allowed European newcomers to retain the familiar network of support and gain access to the potential prosperity and freedom available only in North America.[84]

The *practice* of settlement on the Great Plains and prairies therefore did not produce a wild, unkempt garden where one could not distinguish one transplanted species from another. In both the Canadian and American gardens, each subspecies remained clearly distinct, with each specific variety initially separated, with generous space between them. Time alone would produce the cross-fertilization and introduction of hybrids that fostered the distinctive American and Canadian cultures we know today. It was, however, these early settlement patterns in the late nineteenth and early twentieth centuries that created two of the greatest challenges for schools in the Canadian west – how to teach and assimilate the "new Canadians" on the one hand, and the resulting need for rural school consolidation on the other. Not surprising, Saskatchewan's educational policy makers borrowed extensively from their American cousins in confronting these two great obstacles to a unified society.

Opposing the plans of Saskatchewan's education policy makers were settled, cohesive, immigrant communities, which viewed the schoolhouse, the school board, and their own power as creators of these democratic entities (namely, the "people" themselves) as the bastions of local control. Schools were intensely political entities then, as they are now, and maintaining some semblance of local influence over the teacher's hiring, the school's location, and the program of study inhibited control by the outside "expert" – that individual so central to Progressive movements in education across the North American Great Plains and the larger continent.[85]

The transfer of Midwestern and US Plains culture to Saskatchewan occurred over approximately two decades, roughly from the turn-of-the-century "end" of the American frontier until large-scale settlement wound down on the Canadian prairies in the mid-1920s. It involved a variety of forms, specifically immigration, the flow of US publications and organizations across the forty-ninth parallel, the sociological tour, and the influence of people studying in US colleges and universities. American popular culture also appeared in Saskatchewan through a variety of media.

American culture was so warmly received in Saskatchewan largely because the Canadian west and the American west were part of the same environment – an environment that changed when one crossed west of the ninety-eighth meridian, but not when one crossed the forty-ninth parallel. Economics linked these agricultural hinterlands. What happened in one strongly influenced the other. If Saskatchewanians sought solutions to their distinctly prairie problems, they needed only look south for a viable solution. This was all made easier because in both the American and Canadian milieus the east, and much of what it represented, was something to vilify, not copy. Cultural affinity, as witnessed in the meaning, practice, and language of democracy, the east, and the west, will produce largely identical policy solutions to identical problems. This is particularly true in the fields of both K–12 and higher education.

PART TWO

Forging Saskatchewan Education

US Contributions to K–12 Education Policy

THE HISTORY OF EDUCATION POLICY IN SASKATCHEWAN FOR kindergarten through grade 12 from 1905 until the beginning of the Depression in 1930 is predominantly one of rural schooling. The paramount challenge was to educate a burgeoning population more heterogeneous than any other province, in a pioneering landscape that was harsh, remote, and unforgiving. Into this frontier territory settled hundreds of thousands of immigrants, most of whose mother tongue was neither English nor French. In Saskatchewan, they sought the freedom and promise of a continental frontier that the federal government identified as the "last best west." Saskatchewan's policy makers looked in the only direction that offered relevant experience and guidance – south. American education was in the midst of reform, in response to a "rural school problem" that started about 1880. To deal with parallel problems, Saskatchewanians adopted parallel solutions. Rather than looking east for inspiration, between 1905 and 1930 they looked south to American forms of school reform.

Throughout this chapter, I retain William H. Sewell, Jr's, framework of culture and its transfer that we explored in chapter 3. The transfer of American meanings, practice, and language of school reform to Saskatchewan was part of a larger transfer of culture from the Midwest and Plains states. In *practice*, American methods entered the Saskatchewan system in five related ways:

the hiring of US-trained teachers; dependence on American text-books for normal school (teacher's college), most notably in peda-gogy and the philosophy of education; normal school instructors' pursuit of graduate education at the two major American centres associated with education reform: the University of Chicago and ·Teacher's College at Columbia University in New York; numerous US sociological tours by educators and educationists; and students' use of a great many schoolbooks written and published in the United States. When writing of practice, I emphasize practice at the level of the policy maker and educational elite.

The transfer of American *meanings* to Saskatchewan education is a somewhat more difficult concept to grasp and is the focus of chapter 5, which looks at the arrival in Saskatchewan in 1916 of Dr Harold Foght, the American expert on rural education, and his epochal work in the province. Foght's *Survey* ushers in a language of school reform known as *social efficiency*. Following its dissemination in 1918, the new dialect of social efficiency, and administrative progressivism for that matter, assume a dominant place within the body of literature occupied within the annual reports of Saskatchewan school inspectors, replacing the more traditional language of schooling emphasis on citizenship and the Canadianization of recent immigrants. While I reserve that discussion for chapter 5, many textbooks for Saskatchewan's normal schools betray a similar penchant for matters of efficiency.

Chapter 6 considers US models of *practice* and *meaning* – especially in the distinctive new service university – for the emerging University of Saskatchewan. And chapter 7 highlights the Jeffersonian and populist *meaning* of education in the province's schools and university. This chapter looks at how US educational practice entered Saskatchewan schools, sketches in parallel developments in Alberta, and assesses the degree to which Progressive-style reforms actually influenced the province's classrooms.

TRANSPLANTING US EDUCATIONAL PRACTICE

Saskatchewan education imported American practices through at least five avenues: US-trained teachers, teachers training with US models, normal-school instructors who went south for graduate studies, the sociological tour, and American textbooks.

American-Trained Teachers

The Department of Education in Saskatchewan experienced perpetual shortages of teachers in the decades following the province's entry into Confederation – not surprising in the light of the rapid increase in population. Between 1906 and 1911, the number of school districts increased on average at a rate of over one for every teaching day![1] As families from across Europe and the United States entered Canada's hinterland, the demand for qualified teachers who could "Canadianize" the foreigners quickly outstripped supply. The province initially produced only a trickle of teachers. As well, in this era teachers resigned, married, and quit the profession and/or left the province at a high rate, which drastically reduced numbers. Each year, normal schools granted provisional and interim certificates to teachers whose professional qualifications were incomplete – far more in fact than it did permanent certificates.[2]

The majority of teachers working in 1916 had trained elsewhere, some as far away as Australia. Unlike Ontario some 50 years earlier, which vilified American teachers and textbooks, in Saskatchewan a teacher's national origin mattered little. In 1914, Walter Murray boasted that the educational ideals of Saskatchewan were Canadian and largely Ontarian.[3] By 1930, however, that was no longer the case: education was much more American, and much less Ontarian.

As early as 1911, school inspectors were already seeing fewer teachers from Ontario: "The regulations requiring teachers trained in Ontario to teach at least one year in that province is responsible for a decrease in the number of teachers from that province [in Saskatchewan]. There is an increase in the number of teachers trained in our province; from the point of view of teaching we welcome the increase. As pointed out in my 1910 report, however, the danger of filling the schools with teachers of the 'home' district increases; the discipline, spirit and efficiency of the school is usually diminished, sacrificed to little more than personal or financial interests. In town schools the solidarity and efficiency of the staff are weakened because the work of the school and the interests of the children are relegated to a second place."[4]

A reduction in the number of Ontario-trained teachers, combining with the inability to train enough teachers within Saskatchewan, necessitated a widening of the net to attract teachers from other jurisdictions. Unlike Upper Canada's practices a century earlier, which went to great lengths to do away with republican influences,[5] Saskatchewan welcomed US teachers and others, whom it desperately needed. The department's main concern was not nationality but qualifications. The Annual Report for 1916 observes:

> To obtain each year an adequate supply of qualified teachers is perhaps the most serious problem which confronts the department and which has not yet been solved ... With the 4,481 qualified teachers in charge of schools in 1915 we should have had 6,047 qualified teachers for 1916, an ample supply, because only 179 new schools were opened during the year. The records show, however, that we were compelled to issue 785 provisional certificates or "permits" for periods varying from two to eight months each to keep the schools in operation ... The causes for the shortage are due mainly to the great demand for help in other lines of work and to the fact that many of our lady teachers marry. The war, too, has robbed the province of practically all the physically fit young men teachers. The shortage is felt mainly in our rural school districts.[6]

The document also confirms that the importing of teachers had declined significantly since 1906, when 66 per cent of new instructors came from other provinces. By 1916, the figure was 25 per cent.[7]

By 1920, with the Great War over and life on the prairies returning to pre-war conditions, the department began expecting that it could meet demand. Yet it soon realized that teacher transience from one province to another was increasing, thereby reducing consistently the number of qualified teachers in Saskatchewan.

> It was hoped that the remarkable decrease in the number of provisional certificates issued in 1919 was an indication that Saskatchewan

was on the way to an adequate supply of trained teachers, but the experience of 1920 which shows an increase of provisionally certified teachers did not warrant such expectations. The supply of teachers and the movement of teachers from one province to another depends largely upon the salaries paid and it would appear that Saskatchewan salaries must advance before an adequate supply of trained teachers can be maintained. An unusual movement was noted in 1920 in the return of teachers, particularly male teachers, to the eastern provinces. High schools of the east, particularly, are paying better salaries ... Teachers are urgently required and trustees generally are willing to pay the salary asked, irrespective of qualifications.[8]

Each successive Annual Report articulates the same concern, particularly vis-à-vis graduates of the province's normal schools, in Moose Jaw, Regina, and Saskatoon. Supply from those institutions never met demand. It was not until 1930 that the deputy minister could boast: "The province is now training sufficient teachers to meet all our requirements and in this year issued 1,651 professional certificates to teachers trained in the province. The third class certificate has disappeared and the proportion of first class certificates, as compared with second class certificates, is rapidly increasing."[9]

Noticeably absent from any Annual Report between 1913 and 1930 is any concern about the numbers of US teachers in Saskatchewan.[10] As Walter Murray noted, the province encouraged the importation of teachers with suitable qualifications to meet growing demand from schools and their increasing foreign population. "Though much is done to encourage the immigration of teachers, their professional qualifications are closely scanned. So far as their scholastic qualifications are concerned, the department of Education prior to 1912 recognized only certificates granted by other provincial departments in Canada and the British education offices. The professional training of candidates is even more severely scrutinized before permanent certificates are granted. This practically ensures that all the teachers will be more or less of the same type of scholarship and of professional skill, and represent the same ideals of social and civic life. This is a matter of far-reaching consequence, since the schools are the most effective agencies in the Canadianization of the immigrants."[11] Clearly, sufficient training and the capacity to help acculturate new immigrants were the keys to certification. National origin never receives mention in any departmental documents from the period.

From the time the department started certifying American teachers in 1913, no one seems to have expressed concern over their numbers or the sorts of information and ideals they were inculcating. These professionals were an integral part of a system that sought a society not unlike the US frontier states. In essence, there was more common ground between these states and Saskatchewan (and Alberta) than between Canada's west and its east. The need for qualified teachers for a growing population made recruiting Americans both a luxury and a necessity. The number remained consistent between 1913 and 1930, but moderate.

Between 1906 and 1915, the number of American-trained US instructors was 238 out of a total of 4,979, or roughly 4.8 per cent.[12] By 1929, the proportion had dropped to 659 out of 22, 918, or 2.9 per cent.[13] Such numbers do not suggest extensive American influence.

American Models for Training Teachers

However, American texts dominated the curriculum within Saskatchewan normal schools. If the schoolbook was the curriculum, or, as Bruce Curtis suggests, if the information in it became state knowledge, these books helped shape the thinking and practice of training teachers, and later their pupils.[14]

Between 1908 and 1920, each Annual Report outlined the program of study for the province's normal school in Regina. Notably absent were any books or manuals coming from Canada's east. In Ontario, normal school *Manuals* were abundant in normal schools and were the texts for training teachers.[15] Although other Canadian jurisdictions had such materials, Saskatchewan`s department ignored these in favour of many US titles. Again, unlike in Ryerson's Ontario, which had viewed American texts as unpatriotic and un-British, in Saskatchewan a variety of American books influenced the minds and practice of teachers.

In 1908, over half of the books on the reading list were by American experts in a host of fields, specifically in pedagogy and educational philosophy. Most noteworthy was Herman Harrell Horne's *Philosophy of Education*.[16] Horne undertook doctoral work at Harvard under William James and was long-time professor of education at New York University, retiring in 1942. His idealistic philosophy often pitted him against the instrumentalism of John Dewey. Like Dewey, Horne believed that the individual found development and growth only within the larger whole.[17] Horne's program seems to fit into what Kliebard described as *mental disciplinarian* education reform, because of his emphasis on the brain and its exercise.[18]

Also on the Saskatchewan reading lists was the reformer Charles De Garmo, whose *Principles of Secondary Education* carried Johann Friedrich Herbart's pedagogical thought to the province.[19] De Garmo was professor of the science and art of education and president of Swarthmore College in Pennsylvania. As a member of the child-study movement, he was firmly in line with G. Stanley Hall's child-centred, integrated approach to learning, which dominated so much of the early twentieth century, and with other *developmentalists* in American education. In 1895, De Garmo had been president of the National Herbart Society and, at the annual meeting of the National Education Association (NEA) in Cleveland, Ohio, led an attack against the traditional, humanistic education program of William Torrey Harris.[20]

A second child-study enthusiast was also on the Saskatchewan list and very influential. Elmer Burritt Bryan had studied at the University of Indiana, at Harvard, and under G. Stanley Hall at Clark University. By the time he completed *The Basis of Practical Teaching: A Book in Pedagogy* in 1905, he was president of Franklin College in Indiana.[21] He later became president of Ohio University and Colgate University. Like De Garmo's, Bryan's text would inform education in Saskatchewan.[22]

This American sway extended beyond developmentalism into the realm of social efficiency. Standard reading also included John A.H. Keith's *Elementary Education: Its Problems and Processes*,[23] which introduces the budding teacher to a new mode of education reform, one that Kliebard denotes as *social efficiency*.[24] "In light of the social view of education, the process of education takes on significant meaning. The one comprehensive end takes in the multitude of smaller ends that otherwise become obstructions to the process. The material must meet one unswerving requirement, and the process must be judged by its social reference. *Social efficiency*, of the actual and ideal types, is the aim of education, and the process is one of organizing an individual in such a way that he actually and ideally participates in the life of the race" (emphasis added).[25]

Whereas in the American context of school reform Kliebard argues that various interest groups vied for prominence and influence throughout a 70-year period of change, Saskatchewan's normal schools seemed to adopt works from all interest groups into their curriculum, albeit with a lag of 15–20 years between their prominence south of the border and their use to the north. Dewey-style reform – a child-centred, democratic approach to schooling – would take hold in Saskatchewan late in the 1920s. For close to two decades, from the 1910s until well into the 1920s, social efficiency, as I demonstrate below, became the dominant language of reform in the province.

Another prominent American entry on the list was Rueben Post Halleck's *Psychology and Psychic Culture*.[26] Halleck, unlike the other leading American authors, was a school principal, at the very prestigious Louisville Male High School in Kentucky. He introduced a behaviourist approach to the study of psychology and the child, much along the lines of Edward Thorndike. Thorndike's *Principles of Teaching Based on Psychology*, though not on the Saskatchewan curriculum, was in the school's library.[27]

Unfortunate for our purposes, the department stopped presenting reading lists in its Annual Reports after 1920. What is clear, however, is that there were many American sources in normal school libraries. The teacher's exposure to US materials was intense.

Several other American textbooks carry the physical stamp of the Saskatchewan normal schools between 1905 and 1930. Among them were George Drayton Stranger's *A Brief Course in the Teaching Process*, Calvin N. Kendall and George A. Mirick's *How to Teach the Fundamental Subjects*, Daniel Wolford LaRue's *The Science and the Art of Teaching*, and Harry Lloyd Miller and Richard T. Hargreaves's *The Self-Directed School*.[28]

The presence of a wide array of American books on lists of required reading and in school libraries affected many teachers. Even though Saskatchewan's normal schools were struggling to meet the demand for teachers, they produced large numbers of instructors each year, training them extensively with American models of teaching.

Between 1906 and 1916, Saskatchewan's normal schools graduated 5,677 candidates.[29] Having been reared on American sources in their training, these beginning teachers undoubtedly transmitted this learning into their classrooms. Fully two thirds of the province's rural school teachers in 1916 were trained in Saskatchewan,[30] and the proportion was probably even higher in the cities. By 1926, the total number the province had trained was 18,440 people.[31] With teacher training expanding after 1906, it seems clear that most of the province's teachers were very familiar with American methodology and philosophy of education when they first entered the classroom.

Tomkins confirms this was the case when he asserts that by 1922, Saskatchewan normal-school students were well-versed in the "project method" of teaching first developed by the American, William Heard Kilpatrick. Tomkins characterizes Kilpatrick's method as the most publicized pedagogical innovation of American Progressivism and describes such changes in the Saskatchewan curriculum as indicative of interwar curriculum ferment across Canada that began with Foght's *Survey* of 1918. For Tomkins, "Foght's appointment illustrated an assumption, common in the western provinces especially, that American expertise and ideas could, with modification, be applied in a Canadian environment that was not thought to be fundamentally different from that of the United States."[32]

When combining the preponderance of American sources on the required reading lists with the collection of US textbooks available to and in use by Saskatchewan's teachers in training, we see the signs of an inundation of American practice and philosophy into the classrooms of the province. Teachers had absorbed American methods and thinking about education in normal school. Because a number of their instructors were pursuing US graduate study, their exposure to American models of teaching intensifies still further.

Normal-School Instructors in US Graduate Schools

The 1920s witnessed many more members of Saskatchewan's educational elites travelling south to pursue advanced degrees at the two Meccas for Progressive education reform – the University of Chicago and Teacher's College, Columbia University.[33] Each of the educators below worked in teacher's education at the normal school in Saskatoon or Regina (there was a third in Moose Jaw).[34] From Saskatoon, J.W. Hedley, on staff, completed his MA in 1919 and his PhD in mathematics at Chicago in 1924; Miss Hiltz, director of Household Science, resigned in 1919 to study at Columbia; Miss M.A. Bell, head of the same department, attended Chicago, receiving a bachelor's degree in 1922; and Miss Grayson took leave the same year to resume her studies at Columbia. From Regina, instructors Miss Lindenburgh and Miss McGill studied at Columbia in 1924, as did Miss McLenaghan of the Household Science Branch; Principal F.M. Quance completed his PhD in educational psychology at Columbia in 1925; and two other staff members attended Teacher's College there with him that year. And in 1926, several school inspectors took summer post-graduate courses at American universities.

As we saw in chapter 3, the pursuit of advanced education abroad is one of the surest methods of importing foreign culture into the home culture. On their return to Saskatchewan, these instructors shared their newfound learning with thousands of Saskatchewan teachers, thereby affecting teachers' practice across the province's schoolrooms. These more formal and long-lived exposures to American educational practice and theory were a prominent means through which US methods transferred to the province.

The Sociological Tour: Looking for American Solutions

Though of shorter duration, the sociological tour was another path along which American habits made their way northward to the Canadian prairies. In the decade preceding the First World War and particularly following the war's cessation, the challenges facing Saskatchewan were largely identical to those of its southern Plains neighbour. Given these parallel environments, Saskatchewan's school inspectors were particularly interested in learning about school reform through, for example, attending annual meetings of the US National Education Association. Although the Saskatchewan Education Association was formed in 1907 as a provincial subsidiary of the Canadian Educational Association and the NEA, its role in the province was minimal.[35] For this reason, Mr A. Kennedy, inspector of schools for the Weyburn area in southeastern Saskatchewan, was perhaps the most noteworthy of "tourists" south of the border. In both his 1910 and 1911 reports to the provincial minister of education, he cites speeches he made at the annual NEA's conferences. He strongly endorsed the Progressive practice of industrial education, confirming that the end of education, as he learned in the United States, must be vocational.[36]

Kennedy also attended the 1918 gathering, but played a much more vocal role. He told the assembled delegates:

> Mr. President – The Department of Education of the Government of the Province of Saskatchewan fully appreciates the value of the National Education Association and has requested me to carry to you a message of greeting and good-will. Problems that present themselves to you for your consideration and solution also present themselves to us; and your discussion and solutions are of very great benefit to us.
>
> Through the courtesy of your Bureau of Education and your Commissioner of Education we have recently had the valuable services of Dr. H.W. Foght in conducting an Educational Survey from which very material benefits are expected. I beg to take this opportunity of expressing our gratitude in this connection.

> As our two countries lie side by side; as our boys are fighting side by side; as these two flags can hang side by side, I see no reason why our educational forces cannot work side by side.[37]

A standing ovation followed, as he reported to the minister. The issues facing Saskatchewan educators were indeed very similar to those confronting their US Plains counterparts. The need for greater emphasis on vocational education, one of the hallmarks of the US Progressive movement, was a constant theme on the Canadian prairies as well. In his 1918 report, the American expert on rural education Harold Foght called for greater access to agricultural education: "The entire survey report constitutes a report on vocational agricultural education to the extent it seeks to relate all education in the province definitely to the basic occupation of the people."[38] Such pronouncements were not lost on school inspectors such as Kennedy, who, in his yearly report to the minister stated that developing vocational models in agricultural education like those in Georgia, Iowa, Minnesota, North Dakota, and Wisconsin, might well make agricultural education in Saskatchewan more efficient.[39]

Previously, in 1914, Kennedy attended the NEA annual convention as well as the School Garden Association of America's convention from July 4 to 11 in St. Paul, Minnesota. There he was inspired by what he found and reiterated his affinity for greater openness to American practice. "The three prairie provinces might well extend an invitation to the NEA to hold its annual convention in one of our Western cities in 1917, or later; the inspiration and educational stimulus would prove of inestimable value."[40] In regard to school gardens, he boasted: "I believe the school garden at Souris School, Weyburn, will rank as one of the best school gardens operated in America in 1914."[41] Although Kennedy was not the first Saskatchewan education policy maker to head south for guidance, he was probably the most frequent sociological tourist and the keenest supporter of American methods.

Other elite educators took Kennedy's advice seriously. By 1919, the province had appointed a director of household science, itself a key component of vocational education. The director, Fannie A. Twiss, submitted her yearly report to the minister of education from

New York City, extending her appreciation for the year's leave to continue her studies at Columbia. She had previously travelled to the United States in 1916, visiting Chicago, Indianapolis, and the University of Minnesota to witness household science education there. Similarly, in the summer of 1919, the director of Rural Education Associations attended the NEA's summer meeting in Milwaukee, Wisconsin; spent several days in Madison; visited Northwestern University, the University of Chicago, Iowa State College, and Iowa Teacher's College; and spent time in Minnesota – all to acquire expertise in vocational education and the "rural school problem."[42]

Teachers from Saskatoon School District No. 13 were also frequent visitors to the United States for training in the manual arts. In 1923, Miss Isbister received leave before the school year was over so that she could make her way to Chicago for a summer course. She taught domestic science within the division and was one of a burgeoning group of teachers in that field of study, at both the elementary and the high-school levels.[43]

In his 1926 annual report to the minister, Inspector McKechnie of Regina articulated the changing conception of education in Saskatchewan, highlighting the influence of the Dalton and Winnetka plans on practice in the province.[44] In 1930, the inspector for the Saskatoon School Division, one of the few urban school districts, reported that two local teachers had made the pilgrimage to Winnetka, Illinois, to study the Winnetka Plan.[45] Each subsequent summer, another two teachers made the trek. By the early 1930s, several Saskatoon instructors had taken the summer course at Winnetka[46] and attended a summer study session under Dr Carleton Washburne.

The Winnetka Plan, which Washburne had developed at Dewey's Laboratory School, University of Chicago, in 1919, arrived in Saskatoon a full decade after its US introduction into public education. It emphasized student-centred, individualized, ungraded learning, in opposition to the structured system of grades, ubiquitous throughout North American schools. Washburne's plan clearly established what he described as "common essentials" – those skills and knowledge all students needed in a modern society.

The student pursued these essentials in the "tool subjects" such as math, grammar, and spelling, in an ungraded environment, making progress at his or her own pace. Work in these subjects occupied one half of each student's day, with the other half devoted to a "surrogate experience" in a simpler, community life, largely centring around play and free activities.[47] Washburne's pedagogy represented a break from the routine that policy makers and writers on both sides of the border so often criticized. The lag between its introductions in American schools and in Saskatoon's was standard for such transfers.[48]

◇◇◇

When it was impractical for Saskatchewan educators to tour south for inspiration, often Americans would tour northward to spread the word of American innovations. In the summer of 1919, for example, as Saskatchewan educators attended a summer institute, they were treated every evening for a week to lectures by Professor J.B. Arp, superintendent of schools in Jackson County, Minnesota.[49] Arp was a disciple of Elwood Cubberly and a staunch proponent of school consolidation to ensure efficiency in education. His lectures coincided with dissemination of Foght's 1918 recommendation about the same theme.

Similarly, Carlton Washburne, the architect of the Winnetka Plan, visited Saskatchewan in 1929 at the invitation of Superintendent McKechnie of Regina. Historian Robert S. Patterson suggests that the purpose of the visit was not to encourage adoption of the plan's practices, but rather to keep school inspectors abreast of educational developments elsewhere. Regardless, Washburne's journey stimulated return sociological tours to Winnetka and some experiments with more individualized instruction, largely in urban school divisions such as Regina and Saskatoon.[50]

Taken in isolation, any one of the four modes that we have considered so far in which American educational influences affected teaching in Saskatchewan – American-trained teachers, teachers learning with US models, normal-school instructors studying at Chicago and Columbia, and sociological tours – had a modest impact. In concert, however, that influence becomes profound. A few hundred US-trained teachers scattering around the province represented a small portion of the teachers' workforce, their influence fragmentary at best. But thousands of would-be teachers at Saskatchewan's normal schools studied under educationists who received advanced training at Chicago and Columbia. In the process, they spent many hours poring over the chronicles of US reform efforts that filled the library shelves there. And for school inspectors (who guided those most responsible for implementing education policy) and other officials in the Department of Education, the sociological tour became a further conduit for importing American practice.

American Schoolbooks

As if to complement this transnational exposure, student texts also contained a strongly American flavour. In chapter 1, I was critical of the narrow historiography of Canadian education. One exception to this weakness exists vis-à-vis the history of school textbooks in circulation in western Canada in the early twentieth century. Numerous regional historians have examined their content. The presence of American texts in classrooms seems a non-issue – the province legislated the free distribution of Canadian *Alexandra Reader*s to all school-age children beginning in 1908, replacing them later with another Canadian reader. Closer examination, however, suggests that the *Alexandra Reader*s were not so Canadian as lawmakers originally thought, as emerges in a brief but high-spirited debate in 1909 in the legislature about the contract to procure the *Readers*. Furthermore, although the province intended it to be the reader for all Saskatchewan schools, apparently a number of other American readers infiltrated classrooms for a variety of reasons between 1908 and 1930. Regardless, the presence of US readers and textbooks did not concern the makers of provincial education policy, particularly since most domestic textbooks came from Ontario, were more expensive, and paid little homage to the experiences of westerners on the frontier. The moral and ethical fibre of the textbook was seemingly what mattered most to policy makers, not their national origin. Again, this is unlike Ryerson's Ontario, some five decades earlier, where any republican sentiments in school texts horrified observers. Like American teachers in Saskatchewan schools, US textbooks fulfilled a need that other sources could not.

The departments of education in Alberta and Saskatchewan authorized the purchase and free distribution of the *Alexandra Readers* to all pupils beginning in 1908. These volumes remained the authorized textbooks until 1922 and were a curricular staple for an entire generation of children.[51] Much like the *Irish National Readers* that Ontario used in the mid-nineteenth century, they not only helped a new generation of young Canadians learn how to read, but inculcated new citizens with the political and moral ideals of a fledgling democratic nation.[52] Because textbooks were and are more than a source of information – because the lessons in them represent what a society hopes to replicate in its people – the process of choosing and distributing them is both interesting and informative. Saskatchewanians rarely mentioned content, but expressed moral alarm regarding the manner of the department's contracting with the Morang Educational Company of Toronto. The textbook issue is a further indication that American moralism, as Daniel J. Elazar identified it, reached Saskatchewan.

In January 1909, Leader of the Opposition F.W.G. Haultain, former premier of the Northwest Territories, asked in Saskatchewan's legislative assembly about the government's textbook contract with Morang. He suggested that the American Book Company in New York would be filling the order, and he described it as one of the most corrupt companies in the United States.[53] The books, he argued, were costing roughly 40 per cent more, though less expensive to make, than similar readers that Canada produced.[54] Similarly, Morang submitted the tender for the contract late, but the government still accepted it. "He (Haultain) repeated that it was a profligate and improper deal. There were degrees of graft and while [Commissioner of Education] Mr. Calder might be in a state of semi-purity by keeping free from personal graft there was graft in the deal and there was no question this was allowed with the personal knowledge of Calder ... The books were being printed by non-union labour in one of the biggest 'scab' offices in the country ... Even campaign literature was coming from Toronto and it was quite possible that they (the Government) were getting that thrown in with the free text books."[55]

The *Journal* for the legislative assembly reported similar accusations by Haultain in a *Regina Leader* article on 16 December 1908: "I did not accuse the Commissioner of Education of grafting. I said there was graft and there was graft, but I did not say that the Commissioner had grafted by putting money in his pocket but by violating his public trust and allowing other people to secure undue profits at the public expense."[56]

Haultain's criticisms are difficult to substantiate. The legislature handed the matter over to a committee for review, but no report ever appeared. A brief examination of the *Reader*s themselves does betray American spellings – rather odd in an Ontario printing.[57] Regardless, the outcome of the controversy seems to me less important than its substance. The debate ignored the presence of American readers in the province's schools.

The fact that the leader of the opposition articulated concern over the manner in which an American company secured the contract and about the moral and ethical qualities of Morang itself is most revealing. Haultain's consternation emerged not because of Morang's affiliation with an American company, nor over the existence of US spellings in a Saskatchewan textbook, but because of the American Book Company's reputation (in Populist lingo, it represented "the interests") for using scab labour, its notoriety in providing illicit campaign funding, and the possibility that provincial officials might have benefited financially from the contract with Morang. In other words, textbook content, at the centre of Ontarians' concern over American influence some 80 years earlier, was not the issue at all. The ethics and morality of the government's actions were paramount.

Such pronouncements by the opposition leader reflect the attributes of Elazar's *moralistic* political culture that originated in the American Midwest and Plains: "There is a general insistence that government service is public service, which places moral obligations upon those who participate in government that are more demanding than the moral obligations of the marketplace. There is an equally general rejection of the notion that the field of politics is a legitimate realm for private economic enrichment. A politician may indeed benefit economically because of his political career but he is not expected to profit from political activity and in fact is held suspect if he does."[58] Whereas some political cultures, such as the individualistic, tend to turn a blind eye to corruption, moralistic cultures show less tolerance. This, argues Elazar, ensures greater amateur participation in politics.[59]

Given the moralistic orientation of Saskatchewan's political culture, it is not surprising that the *Alexandra Reader*s became the first choice of the provincial government. According to Nancy Sheehan, their "hidden curriculum" focused on an ethical life. "Political, moral and social concepts included in the selections undoubtedly helped shape the average child's view of the world and his place in it. Perhaps the moral tone was the most obvious. A perusal of these texts showed that a life based on the golden rule and Judaeo-Christian traditions was stressed. Included in the selections were the virtues of persistence, obedience, and truthfulness."[60] Such virtues transcended provincial and national boundaries. The national origin of any particular idea or educational policy was less important than its moral outcome on the population.

In authorizing the *Alexandra Reader*s for free distribution to Saskatchewan's growing school population, the Department of Education was not rejecting a pro-British attitude in its education of an ever-increasing immigrant population. In fact, the books contain a great deal of British and European history and literature.[61] What they display, however, is greater openness to American ideas, methods, and materials than had been possible in other provinces. What had drawn the ire of *traditionalists* in other provinces, namely the prospect of US republican influence, was now obvious in Saskatchewan without concern from the government or its population.

Each year, the department shipped *Alexandra Reader*s to all the schools, thereby standardizing instruction across the hundreds of local divisions. While the distribution of other readers is unclear, the number of *Reader*s the department shipped never equalled the number of pupils in the province. For example, in 1908, the first year it authorized them, it shipped 51, 693 copies for only 47, 086 students.[62] In 1916, it sent out 73,688 to 125, 590 enrollees, and in 1917, 92, 953, for 138, 731 pupils.[63]

This falling proportion has several possible explanations. Undoubtedly, each year a number of students "handed down" *Reader*s to siblings or other family members as they made their way through grades and *Reader*s alike, thereby reducing the quantity of new books that schools required each year. Similarly, as attendance could be sporadic, particularly in rural school divisions, relatively high failure rates were common, making new *Reader*s unnecessary. The presence of other readers in schools also reduced need for *Alexandra Reader*s. It is not clear which readers were in circulation, when, and where, but it is likely that a variety of American products made their way into classrooms, at the very least as a supplement to the *Alexandra Reader*s.[64]

In addition to concerns around the contract to print the *Alexandra Readers*, a second problem probably resulted in other schoolbooks taking their place. By 1911, *Alexandra Readers* were disappearing from schools and children's hands rather quickly. Furthermore, some were in tatters, and school inspectors report each year that they themselves ordered destruction of many copies.

> It is my opinion that a change is necessary in the manner of distribution of the free [Alexandra] readers. It is found to be next to impossible to keep the record satisfactorily owing to frequent changes of teachers, pupils being allowed to carry books home and to keep them at home during the winter ...

> Give each pupil a new book upon entering the grade, to be absolutely his own book, to do with as he sees fit. He could not get another except by purchase.

> *I have this summer sanctioned or rather ordered the destruction of hundreds of books, all of which were abominable and totally unfit for*

use and the unfortunate part of it was that a large number of them had passed through the hands of two and sometimes three pupils.

Think of the sanitary effect.

Think again of the moral effect when a little child is handed such a book and compare with the delights of a new clean book [emphasis added].[65]

While it is impossible to prove that American readers took the place of the filthy and destroyed *Alexandra Reader*s, it is obvious that a host of them were readily available to classroom teachers.

The most noteworthy of the American entries was *The Young and Field Literary Reader,* by Ella Flagg-Young, the noted American Progressive instructor and teacher in the Dewey Laboratory School in Chicago.[66] In the period following the Great War, the *Beacon Fifth Reader* promoted American military success.[67] Inside its front cover was a full-colour picture showing a procession of American servicemen marching triumphantly through a town square as one of them carries the Stars and Stripes, while several American flags drape from windows in the town. Following the picture, is H.H. Bennet's poem *Hats Off!* which implores onlookers to do just that – remove their hats to honour the flag of "a nation great and strong." The *Wheeler's Graded Literary Reader*s pursued similar pro-American themes.[68] *New Barnes Reader*s and *Winston Reader*s also appeared in Saskatchewan.[69] The sort of content that Ryerson had decried as unpatriotic and un-British was readily accessible in Saskatchewan schools around the time of the First World War.

In identifying those school readers that served as supplements to the *Alexandra Reader*s, I am in no way suggesting that the Department of Education sought to promote American ideals in opposition to those of Canada or the British Empire. There was emerging, however, a change in what Sol Cohen identifies as the "language of educational discourse."[70] Because of Saskatchewan's political cultural affinity with a number of Midwestern and Plains states, and common bonds of reform within the larger populist and Progressive political crusades, educators in Saskatchewan "turned away" from British and Ontarian educational practice and "turned towards" that emanating from the United States.[71] It is my belief that political orientations were the main reason for this shift.

It is also true, however, that many Canadian textbooks were often woefully inadequate. Those that Saskatchewan authorized for use in schools often had little, if anything, to say about Canada's west, let alone about the people who settled there. The most telling example is a history textbook that the four western provinces used from 1907 to 1924 – *The Story of the Canadian People*.[72] In it, the story of the Canadian people is one that begins and ends in eastern Canada and bears little relationship to the experiences of those on the western frontier. By 1920, a new chapter, apparently an after-thought, included an eastern Canadian perspective on western Canada, largely about the Red River Uprising and the Riel Rebellion.[73] Because of this dearth of information on the experience of the western Canadian, it is little wonder that educationists in Saskatchewan looked south rather than east for their educational models and ideas. The American Progressive movement in education provided ample footing on which to base an educational system in Saskatchewan following the First World War.

PARALLEL DEVELOPMENTS IN ALBERTA K–12 EDUCATION

Above I argued that the movement of American educational policy to Saskatchewan occurred as part of a larger cultural transfer from the Great Plains to the Canadian prairies. If that is true, then what unfolds in the province from 1905 through 1930 should also develop in Alberta. This is especially true because most of the Americans who emigrated to the Canadian prairies between 1896 and 1930 settled in what becomes Alberta in 1905. A brief glimpse into a couple of key components of cultural transfer reveals this was indeed the case. For example, just as several high-ranking education officials from Saskatchewan pursued graduate work at major US centres of Progressive education reform, so too did Albertan educationists. G. Fred McNally, superintendent of education and later deputy minister of education, and H.C. Newland, an official with the same department, were described by George S. Tomkins as among Canada's foremost Progressive thinkers and practitioners of the 1930s. While the province employed them, both pursued graduate study in the United States: McNally, at Teacher's College, Columbia University, and Newland and a third colleague, M.E. Lazerte, a school official from Edmonton, at the University of Chicago. McNally studied with several icons in Progressive education, including Elwood Cubberly, William Heard Kilpatrick, G.D. Strayer, and Edward Thorndike.[74] All three of these leading men in Alberta education returned from study abroad to influence education policy at home from the mid-1920s on.

While policy makers in Saskatchewan education turned to the Winnetka Plan to change classroom instruction, Albertans welcomed the Dalton Plan, beginning in 1924. The Progressive educator Helen Parkhurst developed it as a key component of Progressive reform in Massachusetts. This plan encouraged individualized instruction and emphasized the student-centred method of scientific investigation, ultimately encouraging students to work at their own pace. At the beginning of each month, students received a list of assignments. On completion of the assigned work, they could opt for examination. The Dalton Plan encouraged students to manage learning time and plan their work, while simultaneously exercising his or her desire to learn "in his own way and even in his own time." Similar to the Winnetka Plan, the Dalton Plan accentuated the social experience of each task, rather than the task itself.[75] As in most Progressive attempts at education reform, student-centred practices replaced the teacher-directed verbal recitation ubiquitous across the continent. The Dalton Plan initially received a five-year trial in one Edmonton high school. Beginning in 1935, the province, led by McNally, initiated a wholesale revamping of the Alberta curriculum, modelling it on Kilpatrick's project-based approach to teaching and learning.[76]

In many realms of education reform, Saskatchewan and Alberta arrived at similar solutions at similar times. The one obvious exception was the new Social Credit government's fairly rapid consolidation of rural schools in Alberta, beginning in 1935 under former teacher and high-school principal Premier William

Aberhart. Consolidation lagged in Saskatchewan until Tommy Douglas led the Co-operative Commonwealth Federation (CCF) to power in 1944. As I argue below, this lag reflected a substantial resistance from "the people" in Saskatchewan who retained a populist notion of local control over local institutions much longer than their American cousins and western neighbours.

Notwithstanding these attempts at reform, Robert S. Patterson believes that Saskatchewan teachers, especially those working in one-room rural schools, still continued with traditional methods in their daily practice. They did so not in resistance to reform *per se*, but for reasons of practical, everyday survival. Like American teachers, they probably made incremental changes, but often reverted to teacher-centred methods and content in response to the pragmatic necessities of schooling on the western frontier.[77]

CLASSROOM PRACTICE IN AN AGE OF REFORM

Progressive education was one of several North American innovations in social policy in the early twentieth century. It placed social change squarely in the hands of experts. Be it prohibition or temperance movements, eradicating hookworm among the poor and underprivileged in the US south, or reforming education across the United States and Canada, Progressivism attempted to remove politics and influence from social reform. The expert, with science as his or her backdrop, replaced influence and suasion as the driver of change. The ultimate purpose was to remake society in a more equitable form. Although equity remained its fundamental goal, Progressivism symbolized reform from above and generally emanated from well-educated policy elites. Many Progressives met resistance from the people they attempted to serve, who seldom understood why changes were afoot and frequently distrusted the attempted influence from outsiders, who came most often from different locales and strata of society. The most obvious example in education came through rural citizens' resistance to school consolidation, often foisted on them by experts such as Harold Foght or school inspectors and superintendents, in hundreds of locales across the continent.

In classroom practice, American historian of education Larry Cuban provides the most detailed analysis of US teacher pedagogy in the late nineteenth and early twentieth centuries in *How Teachers Taught*. Cuban acknowledges the difficulty in finding evidence of practice in inspectors' reports and within teachers' correspondence. He therefore relies on various other sources of evidence to determine if classroom practice began centring on students rather than on teachers during a time of Progressive education.[78] Ultimately, he finds more constancy than change between 1890 and 1940. He did note more evidence of change among elementary teachers than among high-school instructors. Nevertheless most instruction continued to revolve around the teacher,[79] as myriad factors inhibited reform in instruction.

Because country people possessed democratic means to resist school reform, rural teachers found themselves in a precarious position between the wishes of the people (their students' parents, who also sat on the school boards that hired them) and the plans of well-intended, student-centred experts (school inspectors or Department of Education officials). This precariousness remained especially acute among those who taught in one-room rural schools.

Diane Hallman captures the inherent problems teachers faced when invoking any sort of change to classroom practice. Hallman disputes the common notion that lack of training in child-centred approaches prevented them from changing instruction methods. In her mind, everyday matters necessarily took precedence over all others, particularly the challenge of crowded classrooms full of students in up to nine grades at once. This required preparation and instruction for nine different groups on a daily basis, in all subjects, usually with few resources or materials. Furthermore, teachers had to keep the classroom clean and the stove lit and functioning properly throughout each day. They similarly faced alternating and conflicting expectations from inspectors and superintendents alike who wanted child-centred education, albeit with strict discipline, along with full coverage of the three Rs (reading, 'riting, and 'rithmetic). Moreover, parents' expectations frequently opposed those of inspectors and teachers. Within such circumstances, Hallman quips, teachers sought solace and inspiration from their mothers, not from the educational philosophy of John Dewey.[80]

With these obvious challenges facing teachers in rural schools, it is not surprising that where meagre evidence of Progressive pedagogical reform occurred, it emerged from within urban divisions, such as, the Saskatoon School District, which tried to implement the Winnetka Plan in several elementary classes in the late 1920s and early 1930s. Reporting to the district's board of trustees in March 1930, Superintendent Oulton commented on "the marked improvement in the attitude of the pupils toward their work, and successful results being obtained."[81] He recommended that summer sociological tours continue for Saskatoon teachers to Winnetka, Illinois. While his statement confirms that the plan's individualized, student-centred work was unfolding within some elementary schools in Saskatoon, it is far more difficult to determine the degree of implementation, let alone what he meant by "successful results." Indeed, gauging teachers' work in the classroom is a difficult endeavour, especially long after the fact.

Historians of education struggle to find evidence, either within the archives or outside, for what did occur in classrooms in the first half of the twentieth century. Minutes of school board meetings, for example, tend to emphasize the business end of school divisions, and rarely address method or classroom practice. This lack of evidence need not indicate an absence of Progressive-style reforms, but simply confirms our uncertainty about their existence and extent. It is possible, however, to employ more literary sources to help us piece together a typical lesson on the continental Great Plains.

Pulitzer Prize–winner Willa Cather chronicled frontier life in powerful fiction. Her beautiful short story "The Best Years" takes place set in the southernmost reaches of the Nebraska plains in 1899 and tells the tale of 16-year-old Miss Ferguesson in her second year of teaching in a one-room schoolhouse. Her inspector, Miss Knightly, arrives to observe the class. The geography lesson includes "bounding" (mapping) of various US states, beginning with the eastern states. When the process reaches the Midwest, the teacher asks one student, originally from Illinois, for the classic oral recitation. The young man starts his recitation well, but he quickly falters, and his pants and stockings suddenly darken because of nervous urination. The seeming "best years" for teachers such as Miss Ferguesson and inspectors such as Miss Knightly meant, for thousands of nervous students like the young man in the story, the hell of the oral recitation, which remained a source of dread for decades.[82] For that ritual, the student memorized and mastered subject-specific content knowledge and then presented it orally and verbatim.[83]

Herbert Kliebard classifies such practice as *mental disciplinarian*, equating the mind with muscle. The end result for the student and teacher remained "monotonous drill, harsh discipline, and mindless verbatim recitation."[84] Kliebard adds that such an approach typically appealed to teachers, most of whom were very young and had poor training. Ultimately such methods justified a very traditional approach to instruction, but made schools "joyless and dreary places."[85]

Writing about Eastend, Saskatchewan, about the time of the First World War, Wallace Stegner, also winner of the Pulitzer Prize, recalls a similar experience in his famous *Wolf Willow*. For Stegner, education was largely imported and irrelevant. He echoes many of the concerns of Saskatchewan policy makers from the same period: textbooks came from Toronto and emphasized eastern Canadian and British imperial perspectives, while the history never moved far enough west to be of interest to Saskatchewanians. The poems, he writes, spoke of the fear and cold in the eastern woods.[86]

This lack of a western outlook led Saskatchewan policy makers, as I argue above, to look southward rather than east for inspiration, but not because classroom practice on the American Plains differed from elsewhere in the North American west. It is reasonable to conclude that classroom practices on both sides of the forty-ninth parallel remained largely traditional and centred on teachers. While Saskatchewan normal-school programs, instructors, and textbooks urged trainees to emulate the practice of American Progressives by design, the graduates tended to emulate their southern colleagues, instead, out of practical necessity.

Above, I showed how US culture, including political culture, moved northward from the US Midwest and Plains along longitudinal lines to the Canadian prairies. Printed media – particularly newspapers, professional journals, and, in education, textbooks for teachers and students – were conduits for American educational practice to enter Saskatchewan. The movement of US teachers and textbooks established a distinctive undertone in Saskatchewan education. With the arrival in 1916 of Harold Foght, whom we have met several times above, American culture found a further avenue into the province's schools.

◇◇◇◇◇◇

5

◇◇◇◇◇◇

The "Populist Moment" in K–12 Education

FEW EVENTS, IF ANY, AROUSE MORE COMMENT AMONG HISTORIANS of Saskatchewan education, or from writers of that era, than the arrival of the American expert on rural education Harold Waldstein Foght (Figure 5.1). In 1917, Inspector McKechnie of Regina spoke for policy makers: "The survey made by Dr. H.W. Foght, meant an outside expert viewing our system and our problems first hand. We await with interest his report. It doubtless will sum up the best thought of those who are working each day in the welfare of the province. It should also present educational conditions from new or different angles, based on the comparative judgment of a broader expert."[1]

Foght's *Survey of Saskatchewan Education*, for which he did the research in 1916 and 1917, and which appeared in 1918, marks a high-water point in US influence in Saskatchewan education. It also ushered in a period of unparalleled prominence for experts within the province's school system, as ever-increasing numbers of top educators in Saskatchewan pursued US graduate education in the 1920s. At the time of his *Survey*, Foght was on loan from the Bureau of Education in Washington, DC, and he arrived amid high expectations that he, unlike the province's policy makers, could modernize the system of more than four thousand school divisions.

Foght's *Survey* receives more mention than any other event in early Saskatchewan education among historians of Canadian

Fig. 5.1 Harold Waldstein Foght, while president (1925–34) of Wichita State University in Kansas. Wichita State University Libraries, Special Collections and University Archives.

and Saskatchewan education alike. Among the former, Robert M. Stamp mentions Foght's recommendation that all students pursue an agricultural course of study. Stamp dismisses this proposal as not in keeping with Canada's trend of wartime urbanization and industrialization.[2] The fact that both processes were proceeding very slowly in Saskatchewan's rural, agricultural economy is lost in a macro-level, English-Canadian perspective on rural education such as Stamp's.

The few histories of early Saskatchewan education relate any development, no matter how small or remote, to Foght's *Survey*. For example, Brian Noonan cites a brief statement by Foght on separate (Roman Catholic) schooling as an indication that it was far too controversial for an outsider to make comment.[3] Similarly, Cameron Milner views Foght's concern about the inherent "problem" of educating Mennonites in remote communities as showing lack of sympathy for religious minorities.[4] Both arguments, in my mind, emphasize aspects of the *Survey* that were largely irrelevant.

Jack Funk examines the process toward rural-school consolidation from the early twentieth century until its completion in the 1940s.[5] Funk credits Foght for setting the agenda for efforts at consolidation and concludes that in the 1920s the province's rural residents were not willing to surrender their control over local schools. However, Funk pays little heed to the context for Foght's recommendations. Indeed, no history of the *Survey* relates the author, or the report's content, to contemporary life on the North American Plains – life that was rural, agrarian, and deeply populist.

This chapter examines the *meaning* of school reform across the continental Plains and discusses the emergence of a common language that identifies the rural school as "a problem" and consolidation as its only solution. First, however, it highlights Foght's populist sensibilities and places them within the larger populist movement that spanned the continental Plains.

FOGHT'S POPULISM

For American historians of the populist era such as Jackson Lears, populism evoked a Jeffersonian commitment to the nobility of life on the land. Within this conception of the virtuous farmer lay the belief that the city or town was the site of vice.[6] In 1915, H.W. Foght echoed a similar sentiment: "The most serious problem in American agriculture today is unquestionably that of tenant farming and the land exhaustion that goes hand in hand with it ... The American farmer has never learned the full significance of the statement, 'The land is holy and must not be descecrated.'"[7] Much of Foght's defence of rural schools emanated from his belief that the curriculum, whether in an American state or a Canadian province, was fitted to the urban student. The rural student, then, learned skills that would inevitably take him or her off the farm and to the city. Ultimately, the farm was the site of republican virtue, and the urban school, therefore, its greatest threat. In states such as Nebraska, "Midwestern farmers shared Southerners' distrust of the 'the town clique.'"[8] Other American historians of the populist era suggest that the movement viewed education as the great equalizer in society, able to redress the inequalities of rural education and rural life.[9] Farm life was therefore progressive, not conservative. This belief in the sanctity of rural life was felt in both K–12 education and higher education.

Harold Foght was the son of Norwegian immigrants who settled in Nebraska in 1888 when Harold was in his late teens. Coming of age on the American Plains, surrounded by other immigrant families, Foght witnessed the same sort of frontier rural school he found in Saskatchewan some 28 years later. He attended secondary school in Nebraska and later entered the University of Nebraska in 1893, Iowa State College in 1897, Augustana College in Rock Island, Illinois, in 1900, and the University of Copenhagen in 1900–01, and he finally earned his PhD from American University in Washington, DC, in 1918. His biographers describe him aptly as someone who served education on the American prairie.[10]

Foght's experience as an immigrant from northern Europe to the North American continental Plains is instructive of the experience of many. He and his family undoubtedly brought with them an appreciation for rural life and community and a deep understanding of cooperative forms of production so prevalent in their homeland at that time. When northern Europeans transplanted this stance to the American Plains, it took on a cooperative spirit imbued with a democratic sensibility very different from any they may have left behind in Europe and different from the democratic orientations prevailing in the US northeast. This produced a distinctly western American immigrant stock, but American to be sure.

During the late nineteenth and early twentieth centuries, Nebraska, along with other Plains states such as Kansas and the Dakotas, was the heartland for populist political revolt and farmer's alliances. Populist and Progressive politics would influence a generation of American and Canadian agrarian reformers alike who sought a relationship between government and people different from what the traditional, back-east establishment offered. This sentiment, combining with Scandinavian cooperative endeavour, surely influenced Foght's thinking about the rural United States, and later rural Saskatchewan.[11]

Foght's career in education is diverse in experience yet consistent in locale. Although he assumed many posts, his focus always centred on rural education, especially on the American Plains. In Saskatchewan lingo, he was a *westerner*. In 1910, he was president of Midland College in Kansas. By 1912, he was professor of rural education and sociology at the State Normal School in Kirksville, Missouri.[12] Not long after that, he was president of the South Dakota Teacher's College. In 1913, the US commissioner of education, Philander Claxton, dispatched Foght and two other people to Denmark to study the folk schools there. In 1914, authorities applied his recommendations to rural folk schools in the Appalachian region of Kentucky.[13] From 1927 to 1934, Foght was president of Wichita State University in Kansas; the institution expanded rapidly, with great emphasis on continuing education.[14] Foght next became superintendent of the Cherokee Indian Agency in New Mexico. His career in education and beyond shows a remarkable consistency – he sought to improve the lives of rural folks through schooling.

Foght's earliest writing betrayed this keen interest in educating the people of the countryside. His emphasis on rural school consolidation appeared in his *Rural School Consolidation in Missouri* (1913).[15] In it, he states clearly the purpose behind the plan: "The great reason for consolidation of schools in Missouri must be to give our farming population a complete system of schools doing both elementary and high school work, and doing this work so well that children shall no longer be obliged to go to town to prepare for their life work."[16] Foght soon travelled, on behalf of the US Department of Education, to study rural folk schools in Denmark, preparing *Rural Denmark and Its Schools*, which emphasized how rural schools could help combat the negative effects of urbanization and industrialization in both Denmark and the United States.[17]

Foght admires what the rural Danes had achieved quickly. He describes the "appalling rate" at which urban centres such as Copenhagen rose in the late nineteenth century, but confirms that this tide receded early in the twentieth with the industry of the farmers who chose cooperative production and distribution to resist industrialization. Foght sees Danish folk schools as key to that country's transformation, since they engendered mutual trust for the cooperative enterprise.[18] It is with this belief in schools' transformative power that he accepts the challenge to alter the course of Saskatchewan's education in 1916.

He arrived in Saskatchewan as the politics of agrarian revolt in the US Midwest had reached an apex, with the Non-Partisan League taking the North Dakota legislature in 1916, which followed the federal third-party efforts of both Woodrow Wilson and Teddy Roosevelt in the decade from 1910 to 1920. Within this political context, Foght betrayed his populist roots and appealed to the same spirit in his Introduction to his published *Survey*: "Saskatchewan, in common with the other prairie provinces of Canada, is dominated by people of progressive type – forward looking people, who have shown a striking determination to escape the hindering influence of back-eastern conservatism by taking action before their educational institutions shall become afflicted with inertness, resulting in failure to respond to the changing life of their democratic civilisation."[19] Such a strong statement might appear presumptuous, except that this populist expert on rural education had already briefly studied rural schools in Ontario in 1915. He noted then: "There has been little demand for a radical reorganization of the rural schools in Ontario up to the meantime. The farmers are conservative and cling tenaciously to the old ways. The schools have made sufficient changes to satisfy all except the most aggressive of the rural population."[20]

The same ideological current that prompted Saskatchewanians to follow politics south of the border also encouraged the same attention to educational matters. Choosing an American expert in rural education, rather than a Canadian easterner, signalled rejection of the "back east" conservatism of which Foght wrote and a warm reception for American-style education reform, particularly from the Midwest and Plains.

MEANINGS OF THE RURAL SCHOOL

Rather than depicting Foght's influence across the breadth of Saskatchewan education policy, I focus on three interrelating and overlapping themes. We saw above how the province's educators adopted American *practice*, but here I identify their reception of American educational *meanings* and reform *language* into K–12 schooling, again in keeping with William H. Sewell, Jr's, characterization of culture. I view Foght as an intermediary in the transfer of American *meanings* of the rural school and of a *language* of reform.

In regard to the reception of American meanings of schools, I focus on school inspectors' acceptance of the Saskatchewan rural school as a "problem" requiring, first, solution in theme one, and, second, consolidation as its only solution in theme two. The primary sources I quote below display a common linguistic pattern, as Saskatchewan's policy makers come to share the same language of school reform with their American cousins. This understanding flows naturally into, third, the theme that connects Foght's language of reform with Kliebard's "social efficiency" and Tyack and Cuban's "administrative progressivism."[21]

My separation of quotations into separate themes is entirely subjective; many of the quotations spill over into a couple of themes or, indeed, all of them. I stay true to the language of the time, rather than paraphrase for the reader. This necessitates some rather lengthy direct quotations from primary source materials, so that the reader can assess my arguments without questioning whether I have manipulated meanings.

One important caveat, however. The statements I present are those of US experts (Elwood Cubberly and Harold Foght, for example) in the American context and of Saskatchewan bureaucrats (school inspectors and high-ranking officials within the Department of Eucation). In other words, experts and bureaucrats agreed on the rationale for consolidating Saskatchewan rural schools. In chapter 7, however, I will show how this same meaning did not satisfy the people. The democratic ethos among the rural folk of Saskatchewan, which they imported along with American Plains culture, resisted expert influence while maintaining a Jeffersonian and moralistic conception of local control over local institutions.

Before Foght's arrival in Saskatchewan in 1916, policy makers had an inkling about a rural school problem in the province, identical to the US situation, and that consolidation was its only solution. Foght's perspective on the problem and its solution was obviously familiar to Saskatchewan policy makers prior to his arrival. The legislature enacted consolidation in 1913, but the government by 1917 had made little progress. The choice of Foght as the outside expert, apart from its being a rejection of eastern models of reform, was a premonitory acceptance of his solutions, as he presented them in *The American Rural School: Its Characteristics, Its Future, and Its Problems* (1910). Foght himself stated in his introduction to his 1918 *Survey*: "This is probably the first instance on record of a Government extending an invitation to a citizen in the employ of another country to direct the study of its school system."[22] Foght's *Survey of Saskatchewan Education* was designed to succeed where provincial legislation and the prompting of provincial school inspectors had failed. The government needed the approval of an outside expert, in this case an American expert, to validate its policy decisions.[23]

From largely identical environments frequently emerge similar problems. Within similar political cultures, identical problems may produce almost-identical solutions. Foght confirmed there was a problem, and he legitimated consolidation as its solution. In the process, he ushered in wholesale acceptance of American meanings of the rural school and ultimately a new language of reform revolving around the concept of social efficiency. Saskatchewan policy makers had already adopted American meanings for schools and a largely identical populist language. Before I re-create that conversation as to the meaning of rural schools, however, I wish first to articulate the basic premises of populism, both in the US Midwest and on the Canadian prairies.

Populism in the North American Great Plains

Specifically defining "populism" is, as the Canadian political sociologist David Laycock suggests, a rather elusive task, particularly since aspects of the concept impinge on all major ideologies as they existed in Canada from about 1910 through 1945.[24] In the American context, populism dovetails into various dimensions of agrarian revolt from 1890 forward, including Progressivism, and certainly spills over into Elazar's conception of the moralistic political culture that

pervades the American Plains in that era.[25] Regardless, Saskatchewanians share many key tenets with their southern cousins, all
of them clearly evident in the writings of educational experts as
they comment on the rural school problem, consolidation, and the
meaning of the rural school itself.

According to Richard Hofstadter, American populism maintained a notion of a utopian "golden age" of the past, to which
society must attempt to return – a time of equal rights for everyone, including agriculturalists. Industrial capitalism, symbolized by urbanization and plutocracy, ruined this utopia. Lost was
man's harmony with nature, where nature seemed a beneficent
entity that produced prosperity. Populists believed in a harmony
of interests with other productive classes, including urban labour-
ers, but its conspiracy theory of history produced great fears that
society was near ruin.[26]

> The Populist and Progressive movements took place during a
> rapid and sometimes turbulent transition from the conditions of
> an agrarian society to those of modern urban life ... The American
> tradition of democracy was formed on the farm and in small
> villages, and its central ideas were founded in rural sentiments and
> on rural metaphors (we still speak of "grass-roots democracy") ...
> The American was taught throughout the nineteenth and even in
> the twentieth century that rural life and farming as a vocation were
> something sacred. Since in the beginning the majority of the people
> were farmers, democracy, as a rather broad abstraction, became in the
> same way sacrosanct. A certain complacency and self-righteousness
> thus entered into rural thinking, and this complacency was rudely
> shocked by the conquests of industrialism. A good deal of the strain
> and the sense of anxiety in Populism results from this rapid decline
> of rural America.[27]

Laycock agrees with much of Hofstadter's analysis, particularly in
regard to Jeffersonian notions of participatory democracy where
the people controlled society's affairs. He adds that prairie Canada's
populists maintained a belief in cooperation and community and
a dualistic view of government, where they welcomed the positive

use of state power but flatly rejected power that served to produce or preserve inequality.[28]

Within this populist framework, therefore, an American language denoting the rural school problem and consolidation as its solution became evident among policy makers in Saskatchewan education. More significant, however, the meaning of consolidation and the rural school itself, in populist terms, reveals that a transfer in education policy was part of a larger northward transfer of culture from the American Midwest and Plains states to Saskatchewan.

THE LANGUAGE OF SCHOOL REFORM

American Language: The Rural School Problem

Understanding the role of language within culture is essential to gauging the role of US culture in Saskatchewan education. Foght's *Survey* ushers in the *social efficiency* language of school reform. It spread this new language, and the similar dialect of "administrative progressivism," which came to dominate the annual reports by school inspectors, replacing the more traditional emphasis on citizenship and the Canadianization of recent immigrants. Here I borrow from the ideas of Sol Cohen in *Challenging Orthodoxies*: "My controlling assumptions are these: that language or language systems are a class of phenomena or historical source that can be studied as acts, events, or practices, as real and meaningful as any phenomena in the social world; that the field of education is a single discursive field; that we can track the influence of school reform movements through the diffusion and appropriation of language; and that fundamental change in education can be marked through change in the language system. Which is to say that fundamental change occurs when one language system, formerly marginal, displaces another, formerly dominant, in the total discursive field of education."[29]

David Tyack's history of American urban schooling, *The One Best System*, begins by setting the context for school reform in the rural United States at the close of the nineteenth century. As early as the 1890s, when the (US) National Education Association (NEA) formed its Committee of Twelve on the Rural School Problem, the *problem* was already evident. As would be the case among urban schools in the coming decades, solving the problem required that professionals remove schools from politics, stress the importance of professionally trained teachers, and connect the curriculum "with the everyday life of the community."[30] Among the foremost authorities on rural education and the "rural school problem," Elwood Cubberly wrote in 1914 that adequate rural education was not simply about achieving greater levels of efficiency, but about fairness for all students, including rural dwellers: "The chief reason why this has not been done before now, and the chief difficulty encountered in trying to provide such advantages today, is the conservatism and low educational ideals of the people in the rural communities themselves. Too many farmers have no proper conception as to the possibilities of education, or what is possible for country children."[31]

Although educators such as Cubberly assumed national prominence, others, such as Harold Foght, were making similar arguments earlier. In *The American Rural School* (1910), Foght argued: "All well-informed persons agree that conditions in the rural schools are not to-day what they should be for the proper training of the twelve million boys and girls growing up in rural communities. One half of our entire school population attend the rural schools, which are still in the formative stage. And at least 95 percent of these children never get beyond the district school. The country youth is entitled to just as thorough a preparation for thoughtful and intelligent membership in the body politic as is the city youth. The state, if it is wise, will not discriminate in favour of the one as against the other; but it will adjust its bounties in a manner equitable to the needs of both."[32]

For Foght, the source of the rural school problem was clear: "Attendance is spasmodic; interest poorly sustained. The work can scarcely be called graded; teachers change with each term; and with every such change the children are 'put back' to do over again work of which no record has been kept."[33]

Finally, for Foght and others alike, organization of US school districts impeded reform, particularly when parsimonious, close-fisted locals were in charge: "Many of the evils from which rural schools suffer are traceable to the small district. As we shall see ... local partisanship and jealousy, and often close-fistedness and indifference in school affairs, make the district an inadequate basis for administering school affairs. The local school board is too often hampered in its work by obligations to friends and neighbours who elect them and retain them in office. Such a unit cannot possibly afford to pay for professional supervision. But most important of all, the last word in tax matters should never be left with so small a unit, since two or three influential men are generally able to dictate the policy of the district, and make this narrow or broad in proportion as they themselves are narrow-minded or broad-minded."[34]

American commentators agreed on the problem's sources: an irrelevant curriculum; infrequent attendance; poorly trained and transient teachers; ungraded classrooms with resulting repetition and inefficiency; and unsophisticated and narrow-minded rural residents who took little interest in the school, but wanted low taxes.

American Language: Consolidation as Solution

As easy as it was to articulate the problem, it was even simpler for experts on rural education such as Cubberly and Foght to propose its solution. A host of commentators called in unison for reorganization of smaller school units into larger, consolidated districts. Following the report of the NEA's Committee of Twelve on the Rural School Problem in the 1890s, consolidation, or, as Tyack terms it, centralization, became the solution for the ills of rural schooling and rural life in general. Seemingly no commentator appeared more committed to consolidation than Foght. In 1910, he acknowledged that in the rural, one-room school of the US frontier, consolidation would have to wait. In the meantime, rural teachers had to make the most of the new educational trends and attach schooling to the everyday life of the students.[35] Regardless, for him, "the consolidated school is an illustration of the fundamental fact that if the country people want better schools in the country for country children, *they must spend more money for education and spend it in a better way. There is no other way."*[36]

Other experts in rural education were less patient. In 1912, Mabel Carney, who shortly after the publication of her *Country Life and the Country School* joined the faculty of Teacher's College, Columbia University, couched consolidation within a larger crusade for better, more efficient rural schooling. "The country school, let it be repeated, is the most direct and immediate point of attack upon the unfavourable conditions of country life. Increasing its efficiency is necessarily the first step toward progress. But no adequate degree of efficiency is possible under the existing one-teacher system. The immediate need for our country schools is for an army of far-seeing, heroic teachers who will go forth and impress upon farmers and others the inefficiency of the outgrown system. But the fundamental need is deeper than this. And upon it, educational redirection, service as a community center, efficient teaching, the holding of trained teachers, and all else depend. *The fundamental need of country schools is a change of system, or consolidation."*[37]

Consolidation therefore became the panacea not only for the rural school problem, but for what some described as the problem of country life. Although the frontier school developed much later in Saskatchewan than in the American Midwest and northern Plains, the problem remained the same. With Foght's arrival in Saskatchewan in 1916, its solution, not surprising, became identical.

Saskatchewan Language: The Rural School Problem

Even though rural schools became a problem in Saskatchewan a couple decades after the NEA's Committee of Twelve engaged it in the United States, Saskatchewan's policy makers – both indigenous and those Americans it invited to comment – agreed with their southern cousins on its roots. In 1913, the department's Annual Report stated: "The evils of the present system [of rural schooling] are short term schools, involving a constant change of teachers; and teachers badly prepared for their work."[38] In regard to the work of teachers and trustees, another school inspector agreed with Carney's statements on the American rural school problem: "Whether it is the lack of academic training, insufficient professional training or failure to grasp the tremendous importance of her work, the average teacher is not the important force in the community she should be. I think perhaps an older, more mature and more highly trained teacher would work a wonderful change in our schools. On the other hand, we require more intelligent and progressive trustees. While I know many, probably the majority of trustees have the best interest of education at heart, others are holding office to keep down taxes, keep out rivals, or to propagate their particular brand of ideals. Why should trustees not be required to measure up to certain qualifications as well as teachers?"[39]

Although policy makers recognized the problem, the government still needed the influence of an outside authority, in this case, an American expert on rural schooling, to legitimate their efforts. Foght's insistence as to the problem's existence carried on from where he began in the United States in 1910. As was the case there, the curriculum in Saskatchewan held nothing for the rural student: "The local district does not have within its boundaries what is necessary to make a modern community school. The district school in Saskatchewan devotes its energies to the tool subjects [e.g., math and grammar] almost wholly. Very few pupils complete the prescribed course of study. The schools are not organised to attract and hold the larger boys and girls, and most of the schools are unable to provide the social aspects required of modern education. The district school is unquestionably responsible for the following fundamental weaknesses from which all are suffering: non-attendance of a large percent of the school population; irregularity of attendance; and great wastage in attendance due to lack of interest in prescribed schoolwork."[40]

As for the trustees, Foght agreed with a previous Saskatchewan school inspector: "Saskatchewan has 4020 school districts (December 31, 1917), each in the charge of three local trustees. This makes a small army of between eleven and twelve thousand men. An average municipality has from thirty to fifty or more each. Such an organization is inexcusable. It is unreasonable to expect that half a hundred men can be found in a thinly settled municipality suited by temperament and training to fill all these positions even if the men can be found there ... In many municipalities, particularly in non-English communities, it is entirely out of the question to find a sufficient number of persons suited to hold these important positions."[41]

Even following Foght's *Survey*, the rural school problem continued in 1920: "The department has every reason to feel gratification at the progress in education during the year which this report covers. Our work is more 'rural' than in any other province in the Dominion and this fact alone provokes its own peculiar and difficult problems. Our teaching staff is migratory, preventing continuous teaching of a progressive and complete character. The average area of school districts is probably larger than in any other political unit where public school systems have been established, a fact which contains an implication of inconvenient distances from schools with consequent irregularity of attendance and retardation."[42] Although by 1920 a solution seemed distant, policy makers had known for some time what it was.

Saskatchewan Language: Consolidation as Solution

As early as 1913 Saskatchewan was looking south for its solution to the rural school problem. As Foght suggested in his 1910 book, the one-room school must suffice for the time being, and the province's policy makers seemed to concur: "Considering all the circumstances fair work was done, although there is still great room for improvement. It is only fair to ask that the boy or girl in the country should have an equal opportunity to secure good education with those of the town or city. This is far from being the case at present ... Consolidated schools may solve the rural school problem but the country is too sparsely settled to make their introduction a success at present."[43]

Regardless, by 1915, the province had requested a special report on consolidation to date. Deference for American models was obvious: "In many respects, particularly in regard to regularity of attendance, standards of teaching, economy in teaching and community usefulness, the rural schools of North America have proved to be unsatisfactory and there has arisen what is termed 'the rural school problem.' As a solution of this problem, especially in thickly populated settlements where small inefficient schools have been erected, consolidation of schools has been effected. This has been a common solution in the more progressive of the States and to some extent in Canada. Manitoba, of all the provinces, appears to have made most advance in this respect."[44] The report notes that the majority of residents requesting consolidation of local school districts had US experience of it.[45]

By the time Foght appeared in 1916, his findings were a foregone conclusion. In the *Survey*, he wrote: "The following is a concise restatement of the most important recommendations made in the foregoing chapters: (1) The establishment of [consolidated] municipal school districts in place of the present local districts. (2) The organization of municipal school boards with powers to administer the public schools of the Province."[46] Foght had found the same conditions as existed in his Great Plains home, and policy makers seemed keen on his policy solutions. The province expected his expert word to carry the day in favour of consolidation. He served as a conduit for transferring both policy and culture, helping create a very American dialect of school reform.

Education "Rooted to the Soil": The Language of Efficiency

Like other types of US reforms that moved northward, *social efficiency* entered the province a decade or two following its zenith. Although some Saskatchewan policy makers were aware of notions of efficiency prior to Foght's *Survey*, his report ushered in an era of school reform that went well beyond talk about consolidation. Throughout the 1920s, the language of school reform focused on social efficiency.

My discussion of that language of social efficiency interprets Foght's *Survey* and its aftermath through the lens of two American histories of education. First, Tyack and Cuban's writing about the administration of US schools and schooling, which emerged in the early nineteenth century, casts someone such as Foght as an "administrative progressive" who will undoubtedly propose specific changes to Saskatchewan education in line with those of his US colleagues, such as Elwood Cubberly and Mabel Carney. Similar in process, but somewhat different in outcome, are Herbert Kliebard's "social efficiency educators." Like administrative progressives, they used scientific method to place the expert at the head of school reform. Whereas administrative progressives tended to emphasize the administration and organization of schooling, in Kliebard's history of the American curriculum, social efficiency educators transformed the curriculum. Through the lens of Tyack and Cuban's administrative progressivism or Kliebard's social efficiency, it is obvious that Foght's *Survey* imposed an American dialect on the language of schooling and school reform in Saskatchewan.

For Foght, consolidation of school districts would not only improve rural life (a populist goal) but make schooling and the society it supported more efficient. For an administrative progressive such as Foght, the goal of school reform was to remove politics from schooling entirely, thereby placing the responsibility for school transformation firmly in the hands of the expert. His *Survey* noted that, during the initial debate about school reform in Saskatchewan, the leader of the opposition stated: "The school system must be absolutely and entirely divorced from all politics and separated from all party influence."[47] All his colleagues agreed. Within Foght, the populist reformer did not compete with the social efficiency wonk, but instead worked side by side. Unfortunately for his legacy, Foght's recommendations about consolidation did not survive through the 1920s. However, his language of social efficiency, which he helped introduce to the province in 1918, lasted through decade's end, until it gave way to John Dewey's branch of "social meliorism."

Tyack observes an American movement that began in the 1890s to consolidate schools and transportation for students and to professionalize rural education. This attempt at standardization, like the evolution towards the "one best system"already under way in urban school districts across the United States, attempted to expunge politics from schools and transform country children's social values and vocational skills.[48] This too was a central theme throughout Foght's *Survey*.

The survey movement itself was a central component in the program of the administrative progressives that intensified after

1900. Between 1911 and 1925, hundreds of surveys took place around the United States, reaching into every state in the union. They tended to emphasize the financial and mechanical aspects of education and placed the impetus for reform in the hands of the "authorities."[49] The federal government or philanthropic foundations commissioned the bulk of these state or city surveys. Tyack characterizes these endeavours as "highly prescriptive," promoting reforms that administrative progressives favoured.[50]

Foght's *Survey* was no different. Administrative progressives "shared a common faith in 'educational science' and in lifting education 'above politics' so that experts could make the crucial decisions. Occupying key positions and sharing definitions of problems and solutions, they shaped the agenda and implementation of school reform more powerfully from 1900–1950 than any other group before or since."[51]

Foght's survey was the first such effort, and easily the most extensive, in Canada, with Saskatchewan borrowing the surveyor from Washington, DC. Its report, highly prescriptive and obvious in advance to policy makers, followed the prescriptions of Elwood Cubberly and other aficionados of social efficiency.[52] Although a few school inspectors had spoken the language of efficiency in their annual reports, the language of these documents began to evolve,[53] from emphasis on Canadianizing immigrants and creating citizens to the vernacular of social efficiency.

At various points in his *Survey*, Foght assumes a decidedly scientific and statistical approach to school reform – to the modern-day observer, a tone quite out of step with his substantive arguments for consolidation. For example, chapter 7, "Organisation and Adaptability of the Rural School," examines the ratio of glass area to floor space in the rural school. The author reminds his readers that roughly 10 per cent of outdoor light is absorbed through a window; if that window is dirty, that figure may double or triple. A series of pie charts depicts from where the light enters the classroom. Furthermore, only 32 per cent of the rural schools he surveyed had appropriate lighting – entering either from the left only or from the left and rear. A chart gives the percentage of schools with window shades and cloak rooms, the extent of sweeping and dusting, and so on.[54] Only an expert in education could see these numbers as crucial to modernizing schools.

In a similar vein, Foght tackles "waste" – average attendance and the percentage of students repeating a grade. Although city schools performed better, "City and town officials should take no unction to their souls from the superiority of the urban schools over the rural in this regard. The urban record shows a waste of pupil material that would be unpardonable were it not for the fact that it has been the habit of the school and the community from time immemorial to give no heed to the pupil who leaves school or lags behind."[55]

Foght's ability to cite US statistics put him at a distinct advantage relative to his Saskatchewan counterparts, assuring his role as the expert. Yet the outcome of his *Survey* of Saskatchewan education was identical to that of those he conducted in states such as Missouri: the need for consolidating rural schools, full-year schooling from September through June, and better record keeping to monitor waste and inefficiency. These themes were among the hallmarks of the administrative progressives.

Foght's dependence on statistical analysis and his emphasis on efficiency lead me to analyse the influence of social efficiency in Saskatchewan education following 1918. The language of social efficiency replaced the more traditional language of schooling, which emphasized citizenship, particularly vis-à-vis immigrants in rural areas. Traditional concerns about schooling had a common form. In 1911, the inspector for Yorkton, an area that central and eastern Europeans settled, articulated his problem: "From what I have seen of these foreign people, no matter of what nationality, it seems obvious that more stringent regulations should be enacted in order to compel them to send their children to school. These children are growing up in the same ignorance as their parents and are practically drifting right before our eyes further and further away from that high ideal of Canadian citizenship upon which the future of our vast western prairie land depends."[56]

In 1914, his replacement repeated: "In the evolving of a Canadian national type our school is the greatest factor in the life of Western Canada."[57] By the time of Foght's *Survey*, however, the American penchant for gathering precise information about the efficiency of schools – a practice that began in the 1890s south of the border[58] – would take hold. Kliebard describes social efficiency educators as one of four interests groups that competed for pre-eminence across the entire breadth of American school reform during the progressive era.

> It was social efficiency that, for most people, held out the promise of social stability in the face of cries for massive social change, and that doctrine claimed the now potent backing of science in order to insure it. This was vastly different science, however, from either Hall's natural order of development in the child or Dewey's idealization of scientific inquiry as a general model of reflective thinking. It was a science of exact measurement and precise standards in the interests of maintaining a predictable and orderly world ... The scope of the curriculum needed to be broadened beyond the development of intelligence to nothing less than the full scope of life activities, and the content of the curriculum had to be changed so that a taut connection could be maintained between what was taught in school and the adult activities that one would later be called to perform. Efficiency became more than a byword in the educational world; it became an urgent mission. That mission took the form of enjoining curriculum-makers to devise programs of study that prepared individuals specifically and directly for the role they would play as adult members of the social order. To go beyond what someone had to know in order to perform that role successfully was simply wasteful. Social utility became the supreme criticism against which the value of school studies was measured.

> In a general sense, the advocates of social efficiency were educational reformers.[59]

Foght's *Survey* is a testament to the influence of social efficiency in the author's own thinking and to its broadening influence across

North America, particularly relative to the scope of the curriculum. Like social efficiency educators elsewhere in North America, in Saskatchewan Foght found an entirely traditional curriculum teaching ancient languages and preparing only a few urban students for post-secondary education. Foght invoked a familiar hint of populism: "The high schools and collegiate institutes of Saskatchewan offer almost exclusively the traditional course of study of the eastern provinces and the eastern states of the American union. Economic, social, and civic demands are only beginning to make themselves felt. Agriculture, the one great industrial interest of the province, fills a relatively unimportant role as compared with Latin and mathematics. The high schools of Saskatchewan are meeting the needs of one small group of boys and girls who are going to college or into teaching; they are neglecting the large mass of boys and girls who most need high school education in a democracy."[60] Furthermore, the curriculum needed revamping to present-day standards (American, no doubt) in secondary education.

For Foght, the solution was simple and involved social efficiency: abandon the traditional curriculum in favour of one relating to "present and future problems."[61] In Saskatchewan, the emphasis must be on agriculture: "It has been repeatedly pointed out in this report that agriculture is the chief vocational concern of the province, and that the fundamental vocational training is therefore agricultural education ... The entire Survey report constitutes a report on vocational agricultural education to the extent that it seeks to relate education in the province definitely to the basic occupation of the people."[62]

Agriculture, though not a part of the urban school curriculum, must also reach city schools. "Town and city schools should also be considered in this conception of agricultural life. City people may not be expected to become farmers, but what they do become will depend largely on the agricultural prosperity by which they are surrounded. Practical courses in agriculture, rural sociology, and farm economics in the secondary schools are required to forge a bond of sympathy and understanding between town and country people, and would ultimately place agriculture on the lofty plane which it should occupy in the esteem of all Saskatchewan people."[63]

Saskatchewan adjusted curriculum in response to Foght's recommendations, offering vocational education, household science, the teaching of hygiene, and so on.[64] The Vocational Education Act of 1920 adopted the language of social efficiency, providing "for the instruction of pupils in the following classes of schools: (a) day schools, which shall have an independent organization or be constituted as a department of an existing educational institution, the purpose of such schools or departments being to train adolescents for greater efficiency in industrial pursuits and for the duties of citizenship; (b) evening schools, in which adolescents and adults may receive theoretical and practical instruction in such occupations as they are engaged in during the day."[65]

Although policy makers embraced Foght's reforms implementation was difficult, because most high schools were in cities: "On account of the fact that the basic industry of the province is agriculture, and that our urban centres are mainly assembling and distribution points, the opportunity for technical education is restricted."[66] Regardless, the language of social efficiency dominated the department's Annual Reports through the 1920s.

Despite attempts to alter curriculum, the rural school problem persisted, as did the dilemmas a traditional curriculum posed: "The criticism is sometimes made that our high schools prepare for the professions, including that of teaching, while those anxious to follow some form of industry for a life work, find little to interest them. This has resulted in a direct attempt to broaden the curriculum to satisfy all ... While the number of industries apart from agriculture, is limited at present in this province, there must be many boys and girls throughout the province to whom the so-called academic courses do not appeal strongly, but who would be interested in furthering their studies along industrial lines, if means could be found of bringing the advantages of the training provided by *The Vocational Act* to their attention and of giving them some assistance in seeking these advantages."[67]

Rural education did, however, achieve some success along the lines Foght outlined. Agricultural education expanded in the rural curriculum, as the director of rural education reported in

1922: "While no statistics are available, excepting those secured through gardening projects of the boys' and girls' clubs, there is abundant evidence that school gardening is gradually reaching a stage of more efficiency and greater usefulness."[68]

Foght's sort of social efficiency required a certain depth of understanding by people in education or policy making if the province was to receive or adopt it. While most educationists embraced its spirit, some policy makers betrayed a rather simplistic understanding of the concept. Their language of efficiency seemed to lose something in translation.[69]

Some Annual Reports seemed to want employees to be efficient cogs within the efficient school system. Poor teachers were "inefficient," while those who laboured long and hard were "faithful and efficient servants." The efficiency of any school district depended on quality training for its teachers, longer teacher training, and full-year study for students.[70] Poor attendance because of short school years and/or influenza signalled lower efficiency. School nurses reduced "waste" by nursing sick students back to health quickly. Those boards that took their jobs seriously were keeping their schools "attractive and efficient." Students received commendation for efficiency in areas such as physical training. In 1922, cadets earned "efficiency prizes" in a variety of areas. When Dr Snell switched from superintendent for the Saskatoon School District to principal of the Saskatoon Normal School in 1927, trustees praised his "efficient and careful business administration."[71]

Another prominent American theme that emerged occasionally was intelligence testing in high schools.[72] Revisionist US historians have tended to view that practice as a sorting mechanism to protect the middle and upper classes at the expense of the lower. American educationists, such as Edward L. Thorndike, who proposed it saw it as increasing efficiency by using scientific measurement to decide who should attend university. By 1923, rising attendance rates in high school were causing similar concerns for educators.

The attendance in the high school classes continues to increase steadily, and as intimated last year, financial problems of a serious character continue to face many town and village school boards. It is not surprising that one occasionally hears the remark that too many students are getting into our high school classes. Some people go so far as to say that the municipality and the province are overdoing themselves in attempting to provide education, almost free, of a secondary character ... Many thoughtful people, however, while not opposing free training of an advanced character, would limit the advantages to those who can profit by it. These people would recommend some form of intelligence tests to supplement the regular Grade VIII examinations, and thereby select those really capable of benefiting by further school instruction.[73]

The Saskatoon School District seemingly adopted such a perspective a few years later. In 1928, Superintendent Oulton proposed a program for "backward" students. Using the concept of mental hygiene, he assumed that one to two per cent of students were backward in mental development, with intelligence quotients (IQs) between 50 and 80. He surmised that they would become happier and more useful in "auxiliary classes," allowing regular classes to function more effectively. His plan was to have them devote roughly half their time to study and half to hand work. Their teachers would require special training in Minneapolis,[74] which a number soon took.

Clearly, by the early 1920s efficiency dominated educational discourse in Saskatchewan, as it did much of North America. By 1930, however, another stream of American education reform had replaced it. Robert S. Patterson suggests that by 1929 the province was leading Canada in pursuing a more Progressive curriculum.[75] I would suggest instead that Progressivism, like the general American influence, had existed in prairie schools for quite some time. Although Patterson would disagree with Kliebard on the existence of a bona fide Progressivism in education, he sees the prairie provinces shifting away from vocational education towards a curriculum that emphasized moral values and citizenship, under the dean of the movement, John Dewey.[76]

For example, the 1929 report of the superintendent for Saskatoon highlighted an experiment comparing two grade 1 classrooms.

One adopted wholesale the Winnetka Plan, including all its materials and methods, while the other retained a traditional course of study. The superintendent could report no significant difference in achievement. Regardless, the following summer, two more Saskatoon teachers went to study in Winnetka.[77]

In 1930, the Saskatoon Public School Division began working with a professor of educational psychology at the University of Saskatchewan, Dr S.R. Laycock. Laycock conducted research on the psychological well-being of the city's students using a grant from the Laura Spelman Rockefeller Memorial (she was the late wife of John D. Rockefeller, Sr.) to the (US) National Committee for Mental Hygiene.[78] The work of American philanthropic organizations had been penetrating northward to Saskatchewan for some time, particularly in higher education, and helped shape Saskatoon's university, which became an exemplar of American influence under President Walter C. Murray (see chapter 6, below).

The transfer of American educational practice, meanings, and language of reform to Saskatchewan occurred along many avenues between 1905 and 1930. Teachers practised American models among students who used many textbooks that originated in the United States. Educationists and bureaucrats received American meanings of the rural school and school district reorganization following the dissemination of Foght's *Survey* in 1918, a report by an American expert on rural education whose populist roots permeated his thinking about the rural school. Ironically, at the level of the people, the acceptance of US populist democratic meanings and language of local control prevented the adoption of consolidation until the 1940s. Finally, Foght's *Survey* also signalled a shift in the 1920s away from a traditional language of schooling towards that of social efficiency. Saskatchewan developed its system of education, particularly among rural schools, in ways largely parallel to practices that the US Midwest and Plains had adopted 10–20 years earlier. Parallel development occurred in K–12 schools and intensified in higher education, where, beginning in 1907, the Wisconsin Idea secured its place on the banks of the South Saskatchewan River in Saskatoon.

◇◇◇◇◇◇◇

6

◇◇◇◇◇◇◇

The University of Saskatchewan and Its "Culture of Emulation"

CREATED IN 1907 BY AN ACT OF THE PROVINCE OF SASKATCHEWAN, the University of Saskatchewan became the sole university for a new province that encompassed more territory than North Dakota, South Dakota, and Nebraska combined. It was formed "for the purpose of providing facilities for higher education in all its branches and enabling all persons without regard to race, creed or religion to take the fullest advantage."[1] The institution's first president, Walter C. Murray, decreed it to be a people's university and a servant that would touch the life of the entire province. Although such grand, populist statements might fall fresh on the ears of most residents in a province barely two years old, such democratic utterances were quite common amidst other institutions of higher learning across the continent. Reform in American higher education, which began immediately following the Civil War in 1865, was proceeding well in advance of comparable Canadian institutions. Indeed, many reforms at US land-grant[2] and state universities, particularly in the Midwest in the period 1862–1930, influenced the University of Saskatchewan as it sought to become a "world class institution" in its own right. On laying the cornerstone for the university's College Building in July 1910, Prime Minister Sir Wilfrid Laurier suggested that the institution would one day become one of the world's greatest universities, alongside other great campuses such as Oxford and Cambridge.

History shows, however, that Saskatchewan's first university has instead emulated the University of Wisconsin.

To articulate the influence of US models on the new institution, I look first at American higher education in about 1900 in terms of four major developments following the Morrill Act of 1862, and then at the way the University of Saskatchewan emulated these. In terms of Sewell's attributes of culture, three of these areas involve cultural *practice* – organizational structure, the evolution of academic freedom, and the influence of philanthropy; and the fourth relates to *meaning* – the academic ideal of the university, more specifically the post-Civil War service university.

In the first three cases (and even in the architectural style of its early buildings) the development of the University of Saskatchewan bears striking resemblance to that of its American counterparts, particularly Midwest land-grant and state universities. Specifically, President Walter Murray wished above all to emulate the University of Wisconsin. His University of Saskatchewan became a US-style institution in the middle of the Canadian prairies. The fourth strikes at the institution's *meaning* to the province. It unfolded in a manner identical to that of the University of Wisconsin vis-à-vis its state – it was to be a service university reaching to every corner of the jurisdiction. Unlike K–12 education, however, which evolved through the interplay of meanings expressed by policy makers and educators on the one hand, and by the people on the other, the meaning of the University of Saskatchewan was delivered to the people and their policy makers through the efforts and single-minded devotion of its president, Walter Murray.[3]

THE MODELS

American institutions of higher learning, particularly those in the northeast, developed earlier than their Canadian counterparts and initially looked across the Atlantic for their inspiration. However, some *standard* texts in the history of American higher education reveal uniquely indigenous features that emerged in the later nineteenth and early twentieth centuries. Laurence Veysey identifies three conceptions of academic reform that crystallized at the end of the Civil War.[4] The first borrowed directly from the great German universities and focused on pure *research*. The second demanded a more *cultural* orientation and hailed from Oxford and Cambridge universities in England. The third was entirely American and emphasized *service* and *vocational training*, particularly in applied science and engineering.[5] While most campuses supported all three approaches, the service university dominated by about 1900, particularly in the Midwest. Congress's passage of the Morrill Act of 1862 paved the way for federal financial aid for states creating colleges for agricultural and mechanical instruction – "land grant" universities.

Organizational Structure

Most American commentators agree that this period witnessed democratization of the university. Kerr sees this sea change as representing a populist turn in society that demanded an institution of higher learning that served the needs and interests of the entire state, not simply those of "gentleman scholars."[6] With the advent of Progressivism, the American college curriculum, particularly after the First World War, assumed a technocratic orientation centring on efficiency and a differentiated curriculum.[7] The pragmatic American university catered to the student preparing for a specific occupation or profession, which meant modifying the curriculum and lowering admission standards to accommodate both the practical and the status-minded students.[8] Business and engineering colleges expanded rapidly, as did other professional schools.

In a similar vein, universities organized themselves in a much more efficient and corporate-like structure throughout this period. At the head of the institution was a powerful and often-charismatic leader who assumed the responsibility for most aspects of its academic and business affairs. Aloof from the faculty and administrative staff, this president often unilaterally personified the aspirations of his corporation.[9] The emerging division of labour, with deans running academic colleges and faculties, and with chairs in charge of disciplinary departments, further extended the corporate metaphor. Whether faculty members were shareholders within the corporation, or mere employees of it, became a pressing issue during the period of higher education reform.[10]

To accommodate the increasing demand for higher education, the state universities and colleges assumed greater prominence in most states, as teachers' colleges and the like became more accessible four-year regional colleges or universities.[11] They became democratic institutions of mass higher education as they attempted to meet their states' growing need for advanced education. As more students joined this American "culture of aspiration," as Levine describes it, two-year junior colleges also formed and expanded during the 1920s and 1930s. These general institutions took higher learning to more remote areas, in addition to helping maintain the academic integrity of the larger, academically rigorous four-year institutions by admitting students not quite ready for their rigours. Concerns over too much vocationalism and excessive intellectual diffusion appeared regularly from scholars during this time of curricular reform: "It [vocationalism] deprives the university of its only excuse for existence, which is to provide a haven where the search for truth may go on unhampered by utility or pressure 'for results.'"[12] Notwithstanding these small pockets of dissent, expansion continued throughout the 1920s. Only the onset of the Depression could slow such remarkable growth.

Academic Freedom

Academic freedom within American institutions of higher learning also evolved in a unique fashion during this era, quite different from the German universities whence the concept emanated, and somewhat distant from what many American faculty members envisioned the concept to mean. In essence, American institutions tied academic freedom rather tenuously with the concept of academic responsibility. The result of this tense relationship, Clyde Barrow argues, was a narrow conception of freedom on the part of many presidents and trustees, and an unbridled belief in complete academic licence by the faculty. However, this relationship was constantly under the discipline of the moral and political values of the status quo.[13] The final arbiters in such issues were invariably the founders and trustees of the university, not the professoriate. Although disputes over the extent of academic freedom were often public and involved figures with a high profile, the decisions regarding their continuing *employment* at a particular university took place behind closed doors and were not open to public suasion.[14]

Philanthropic Support

The late nineteenth and early twentieth centuries saw the birth of one further, uniquely American feature: external philanthropic support. Rudolph posits that "foundations surveyed the educational situation in various areas and states and held out the promise of attractive gifts if measures were taken to eliminate duplicate facilities, or to put state systems of financial support into better order, or to consolidate into a more efficient organization neighbouring competitive institutions."[15] Particularly between 1920 and 1940, the Carnegie and Rockefeller foundations invoked standardization and gave large sums of money to worthy institutions, while withholding support from those they deemed unsuitable. Inevitably, the resulting, asymmetrical system of higher education benefited a few institutions at the expense of the many.[16] While American commentators understandably focus on the influence of these corporations on US universities, Canadian Jeffrey Brison confirms that this standardization travelled north of the border as easily as did American scholars.

EMULATING THE MODELS

To borrow Richard Rorty's term, the *vocabulary* of higher education in Saskatchewan was always American, populist, and Progressive. Beginning from his appointment as president, Walter Murray impressed on his board of governors the need for a sociological tour to visit "some of the universities to the south whose problems are similar to those of Saskatchewan."[17] Despite the numerous, well-established universities in Canada's east,[18] he instead looked south for his inspiration. Just as we saw above for the province's elementary and secondary education – where policy makers looked south rather than east – its new university looked to American models. Here the Midwestern state university seemed the most appropriate model for the province's only university. The following section looks at three major aspects of the resulting cultural *practice* in the new institution – corporate structure, American philanthropy, and academic freedom – and then at the cultural *meaning* of the new university to its province – specifically, its use of the "Wisconsin Idea" as a blueprint for its development and practice. But first, we see how Murray definitively left the east behind when he moved to Saskatchewan and started building his university.

Departing Halifax in 1908 on the long trek to the Canadian prairies, Walter Charles Murray was in his early forties, exiting a promising academic career at one of the most prestigious universities in the east. But he was also leaving behind the denominational struggles and local conflicts that plagued many eastern universities. Universities in the east, much more than those west of Ontario, resembled universities from across the Atlantic. Travelling west to take the helm of a brand new institution not only allowed Murray to create a university unlike any other in Canada, but also symbolized his opportunity to re-create himself, free of the burdens of the east.

Arthur Morton credits Northwest Territories Premier F.W.G. Haultain with recognizing that the soon-to-be province of Saskatchewan would need a university different from those in Ontario and the Maritimes. "Too often the institutions of the West have been humble imitations of those in the East. But Haultain's mind was too virile, and his decisions grew too much out of his own experience and knowledge, for him to follow slavishly the example of the older sections of Canada. At this time [1903] he laid down a principle which, followed a few years later, was to make the University of Saskatchewan an institution without its like in Canada."[19] He patterned it after some of the finest state and private universities in the American Midwest.

Fig. 6.1 Chemistry Building, University of Saskatchewan (c. 1925).
University of Saskatchewan Archives, A-3923

This practice of replicating key aspects of US higher education began first with the choice of architectural design for the campus buildings. While on an information-gathering expedition south of the border, shortly after assuming the role of president, Murray and two board members agreed on the beautiful "Collegiate Gothic" design as it existed at Washington University in St Louis, Missouri. The architectural style impressed all observers with its aesthetic beauty. Once they learned that Princeton had earlier adopted Collegiate Gothic architecture, the board quickly agreed on such a style as ideal for the University of Saskatchewan.[20]

John Thelin explains that American universities often chose design that spoke to the values of the campus itself. "Architecture is essential for capturing and conveying the historical motifs that each campus projects via its monuments and memorials."[21] In replicating a particular US campus style, the governors decreed the form and function of their institution, which they decided in 1909 to locate in Saskatoon. By design, it borrowed heavily from its southern cousins, adopting the physical structure of some influential American universities as its own (compare Figures 6.1 and 6.2).

Fig. 6.2 Brookings Hall, originally University Hall, Washington University, St Louis (c. 1902).
Washington University Libraries, University Archives, Department of Special Collections.

Corporate Structure

On their exploratory tour of American state universities, Murray and his comrades undoubtedly encountered at the helm of each a powerful and relatively autonomous individual in the office of president. As Veysey posits in his history of American higher education, this official fulfilled two basic roles, as spokesman for the educational experiment and as manager of a concrete enterprise.[22] These roles often isolated him from the faculty and gave him great power over it. This certainly was the case for Walter Murray at Saskatchewan. "He knew more about the matters than any of the other participants, and he was the only person to sit on board, senate, and council. The constitution of the University of Saskatchewan had made it possible for the president to be strong. Murray chose to take advantage of these provisions."[23] Similarly, Hayden suggests: "Murray's action in 1919 [against the few faculty members who openly opposed him] was consistent with his philosophy after 1908 – the president should be the one man to choose the faculty and divide the money. The faculty could provide advice but was not to be trusted to have the perspective necessary for choosing and dividing. He admitted that the faculty had an important role in the administration of educational matters, and that is why he modified the form of the council. In practice, however, Murray ran the council."[24]

Like Presidents Van Hise of Wisconsin and Hill of Missouri, Murray soon came to personify the university he guided – a patriarch with influence over virtually every aspect of higher education, not simply in Saskatoon but across the province. At the time of his death in 1945, he was simply "Murray of Saskatchewan," so closely did people identify him with the institution he formed over the course of 30 years. In terms of his understanding of higher education, no one in the province could match him. Virtually no one on campus ever questioned his decisions, and the province usually granted his requests for assistance. He so successfully separated himself from the social elite in Saskatoon that he never really had to answer to it, although his aloofness from life outside the university hurt him during the single challenge to his leadership in 1919.[25] But this quickly passed, as the 1920s saw unparalleled growth at the university. As the campus grew, so too did Murray's stature within the province.[26]

The framers of the University Act in 1907 had at their disposal the University of Toronto Commission Report of 1906. Hayden suggests that this document served as the blueprint for the new university's organization. The Toronto plan, however, was itself a mirror of several state universities, including Wisconsin. Therefore the borrowing was an indirect appropriation from American sources.[27] Because many instructors were either American born or had received US graduate training, there was little reason to anticipate much objection from that quarter to a structure that resembled what they already knew.[28]

Of the first five faculty members, two completed graduate work in the United States. In 1910, three of five new hires had completed graduate work in the Ivy League. In 1911, one of two hailed from the United States; in 1913, two of three. In its earliest phase, the university depended on American-trained graduates within the faculty, particularly in mathematics and sciences, since graduate study in Canada was in its infancy. Murray listened to Hill of Missouri: "If I were seeking now, for instance, a man in Philosophy, I should turn naturally to Harvard, Columbia and Cornell. If I wanted a man for English, I should likely inquire of Harvard and the Johns Hopkins, and so on. After you once have your heads of departments, your leading men can advise you as to the best place to find younger men in their line. Though I may be somewhat prejudiced in this matter, I should say that in your situation you would do well to seek for Canadians who have studied in the United States and know something of the conditions in the Middle West especially."[29]

The College of Agriculture epitomized Murray's dilemma. As he learned from Dean Rutherford in 1916, Canadian institutions were not graduating enough men in most fields, but particularly in agriculture, where only the Ontario Agricultural College (OAC) in Guelph, Ontario – an affiliate of the University of Toronto – was turning out scholars. People seeking advanced work in agriculture, Rutherford stated, had to go to Iowa State College (later Iowa State University) in Ames; Cornell University in Ithaca, New York; or the University of Illinois in Urbana/Champaign.[30] Rutherford himself was the embodiment of this need: prior to becoming dean, he had taught at Iowa State College. Indeed, because of Rutherford and others, US Midwest and Plains campuses supplied many instructors in the College of Agriculture.[31]

For example, the college's first professor in field husbandry was John Bracken, a graduate of OAC who began advanced studies at Urbana/Champaign in 1909. In 1913, Murray hired K.G. McKay, a graduate from Guelph who completed postgraduate work at Iowa State College as assistant professor of dairying. In 1916, the college turned to Dr A.G. Hopkins, a graduate of the Ontario Veterinary College in Guelph and of Ames and Chicago, who had served on staff at Wisconsin, to lecture in veterinary sciences. In 1918, Dr Patterson, another OAC alumnus who took postgraduate work at Illinois, joined Horticulture. One of the college's own graduates, a Dr Harrington, returned on faculty in 1925, having completed his PhD at Minnesota.[32]

At the pinnacle of American trainees sat Dr Evan Hardy, who was born in Sioux City, Iowa, and completed his doctorate in Ames. For a generation, Hardy was the mainstay for the Extension Program – another component of the Wisconsin Idea. He also founded in 1924, and presided over, the University of Saskatchewan chapter of the American Society of Agricultural

Engineers. He deferred regularly to the practices, organizations, and standards of places such as Ames and influenced a generation of Saskatchewan students and practitioners of agricultural science. US standards such as Iowa State College's became the norm in the province.

By 1929, the leading surveyor of the campus for the Carnegie Foundation for the Advancement of Teaching reported that 18 of a total of 31 doctorates in the Sciences faculty came from American universities. In total, American trainees had 27 of 61 doctorates on staff.[33] Furthermore, seven of 25 instructors with master's degrees had them from US institutions.

Professors frequently took sociological tours to major US universities or invited US academics to Saskatoon. For example, Dean Rutherford made several trips to the Midwest, including Minnesota in 1915 and Minnesota, Wisconsin, and Illinois in 1918. In 1912, he asked Ohio State University in Columbus for information on five-day short courses and appealed to faculty members from the University of California, at Purdue, and from the Massachusetts Agricultural Station to judge summer agricultural fairs in the province. When Evan Hardy took sabbatical in 1929, he visited the usual tour sites – Minnesota, Michigan, Michigan State, Wisconsin, and Cornell – and also made a stop in Ontario at Guelph.[34] The presence of so many faculty from and emulators of US campuses made it easy to maintain an American structure in Saskatoon.

From its outset, the organizational structure resembled that of most US universities. Dean of Agriculture W.J. Rutherford[35] was second in status only to the president and, unlike other deans, had his residence on campus. With creation of the College of Arts and Science, George Ling, professor of mathematics, who completed his graduate work at Columbia, became dean. As new schools and colleges opened, they gained a dean, and, as specialization increased, departments soon followed. As Barrow would suggest, the corporate ideal was alive and well.

That ideal extended to "branch offices" around the province in the form of junior colleges. Regina College, a consolation prize in 1910 to the province's largest city and provincial capital,[36] remained a subsidiary until the mid-1930s. As Murray wrote in 1910: "We can let it be known that we are benevolent in our attitude to them [the Methodists in Regina] on the understanding that the purpose of the college is as outlined in their petition to the city council, and that they intend to become a feeder to the University and not a competitor."[37] Indeed, Murray favoured junior colleges as a means to limit their capacity to challenge his and his campus's supremacy. By 1929, there were seven colleges, each a private religious school except for Moose Jaw Central Collegiate.[38]

Unlike their American cousins, Saskatchewan's junior colleges were much less vocational and far more religious in focus. Regardless, they did increase access and served a certain utility in a vast province whose landscape was difficult to traverse at the best of times, but especially in the dead of winter. Junior colleges did represent a democratizing in higher education, like their American counterparts that Murray admired for their seeming utility and efficiency.[39]

American Philanthropy

As we saw above, Murray's influence over higher education extended across the province and inhibited any challenges to *his* university's stature. His close affiliation with American brands of higher education, and specifically with the Carnegie Foundation for the Advancement of Teaching (CFAT), influenced his actions in regard to an emerging corporate model of higher education in a land with few corporations.

Murray viewed financial support from the CFAT as essential to gaining Saskatchewan's acceptance into the "club" of North American universities. While on faculty at Dalhousie, he had witnessed at first hand the spoils flowing from association under the Carnegie umbrella, as Carnegie money sought to turn it into a "Scotian Harvard" and made it the most prestigious campus in the Maritimes. Selective endowment, however, created a two-tier system of universities that had some parallels with that in the United States. Those campuses that received large sums of money quickly entered the first tier; the rest stayed in the second.[40]

Murray pursued Carnegie support with zest even before his

first building was complete. Although he persistently appealed for financial assistance, he initially appeared only on the Carnegie Institute's mailing list[41] and received only about $15,000 during his three decades as president – a far cry from the large sums that other Canadian universities received from Carnegie or Rockefeller. Even though he was the quintessential "Carnegie man" at Saskatchewan, his connection to CFAT did not secure his campus a place in the first tier. In his effort to win its support, he tried to replicate American corporate structure and organization, yet CFAT never thought that his university quite "measured up." But in the process, he crafted a Midwest-style campus like those that it did subsidize.

One Carnegie corporate ideal that Murray successfully promoted was contempt for the "inefficient" duplication of services and sharing of resources between competing institutions. Thelin argues that, beginning about 1920, "systemwide efficiency, according to the representatives of the major foundations, demanded that institutional missions be reworked to avoid program duplication."[42] A hierarchy of institutions quickly developed in the United States, with the private universities of the northeast gaining much more philanthropy than their public competitors. In Saskatchewan, this meant that Regina College remained a feeder to Murray's campus, not its competitor. Murray, in a rather clandestine and deceitful fashion, used his influence with the Carnegie Foundation to deny his potential rival resources to expand and challenge his monopoly. Conversely, the Carnegie Corporation did fund a study of the province's "Junior College problem." Not surprising, at least for Murray, it found "that under the existing conditions, the concentration in one responsible state-controlled institution of the authority within the province to issue and evaluate educational degrees is sound and should be perpetuated."[43] Murray had helped transplant the corporate ideal to Canada's west and become one of the Carnegie Foundation's most dutiful representatives.

The influence of American philanthropy is also noteworthy in its absence at Saskatchewan. In the 1920s, the Rockefeller Foundation, through its General Education Board, was founding medical schools in the west. As Jeffrey Brison argues, "Concerns for efficiency and scientific management always dictated Carnegie and

Rockefeller approaches to reforming and/or creating educational infrastructure."[44] Saskatchewan and Saskatoon's small populations made a medical school inefficient. Thus, while the University of Alberta in Edmonton received $500,000 from Rockefeller, and the University of Manitoba in Winnipeg gained $750,000 from Rockefeller, Saskatchewan received nothing. The two pioneers became the model for later medical schools in the region, including Saskatoon's. In replicating the conditions for acquiring a medical school in Saskatoon, along the lines of those pre-existing in Alberta or Manitoba, Saskatchewan was in fact pursuing an American model similar to the ones that the General Education Board set up.[45]

In 1926, the University of Saskatchewan did finally create a "medical school" that provided the first two years of medical training. Students who successfully a comprehensive those years could finish their degree elsewhere at another, *major* Canadian university. In 1956, the campus created a comprehensive medical school, allowing a student to begin and complete a medical degree there.[46] Failure to secure American philanthropy, whether from Carnegie or Rockefeller, therefore had a tremendously stifling effect on the university and left it a *minor* Canadian institution relative to its regional counterparts in Alberta and Manitoba.

Universities in the west pursued American foundation support for a host of reasons. Canada had no comparable agencies, and wealthy philanthropists were few on the prairies. Murray witnessed the benefit of Carnegie support at Dalhousie, where the pension fund for the CFAT helped attract new and talented academics.[47] Murray himself sought influence on the CFAT's board of trustees, which he joined in 1919; he served as vice-chair 1922–1924 and chair 1934–35.[48] He sought Carnegie evaluation of his university to add credibility to its program and focus, and in 1929 the Carnegie umbrella finally welcomed it.

Although Murray could not obtain large-scale Carnegie financial support, he did acquire small grants. A three-year grant began in 1930 to establish a chair of music, which Carnegie renewed for three more years in 1933.[49] In 1931, the university received $2,500 for musical equipment.[50] Finally, in 1935, Carnegie offered $4,500 for a

Fig. 6.3 President Walter Murray at his desk, College Building, University of Saskatchewan (1937).
University of Saskatchewan Archives, A-5537.

guest professor for two years. The German physicist and displaced
scholar Dr Gerhard Herzberg arrived as a guest to escape Nazi
persecution.[51] He remained on faculty for 10 years and continued
his illustrious career at the University of Chicago, the University
of Toronto, and Canada's National Research Council, winning the
Nobel Prize for chemistry in 1971.

While such funding certainly aided the university in a time
of drought and economic depression, Murray's obsession with
Carnegie made it a replica of the American corporate university.
Barrow's Marxist critique outlines the corporate ideal and its influence on the American campus. The University of Saskatchewan's own rationalization fits very neatly into Barrow's model,
which separates administration from operations and depart-
mentalizes and centralizes decision making in a hierarchical
pyramid.[52] This era socialized university presidents to the norms
of the American corporation. As a Carnegie representative, Murray embodied the corporate ideal in higher education,[53] much to

the detriment of "employees" who dared challenge his position. Figure 6.3 depicts Murray in the twighlight of his tenure as president.

Academic Freedom

The "crisis of loyalty" of 1919 is most significant for its outcome, not its cause. Unlike the Ely case at Wisconsin, which emerged over the professor's many socialist ideological pronouncements over a long period, the crisis at the University of Saskatchewan stemmed from four faculty members' public challenge to Murray's accounting practices and what they perceived as his dictatorial manner at the head of the "corporation." The university dismissed the "gang of four," and Murray had a nervous breakdown.[54]

Most significant, the crisis led the university to articulate its practice about and limits of tenure. Following an investigation of the original charges, and then a follow-up on the professors' dismissal, a university-appointed investigator confirmed that the professors worked "at the pleasure of the board."[55]

S.E. Greenway, director of extension work, had gone to the provincial government in March 1919 with the charge that Walter Murray had falsified financial reports and misappropriated funds. He went to the treasurer without speaking to Murray, nor informing him of his complaint. Greenway, the heads of Chemistry and Physics, and one law professor also asserted that Murray no longer held the confidence of his faculty – a charge that Murray and the provincial cabinet took seriously. When the board of governors invited the professors to prove these accusations, Greenway withdrew his request for an investigation and suggested that he never intended to accuse Murray of dishonesty. The three other professors, however, never appeared before the board. The faculty held a vote of confidence, without the four malcontents present, and overwhelmingly expressed confidence in the president. The university offered the four dissidents paid leave, at the end of which they would resign. When the four refused, and carried on as if nothing had happened, it summarily dismissed them.[56]

Even though the board presided over the investigation of the charges against Murray, it was Murray's influence and insistence that carried the day in his favour. He was quite aware of the high-profile dismissals of faculty members at American campuses early in the century and insisted on dismissal or he would resign.[57] Only a man of his stature could so easily turn the table on his accusers. His reputation in higher education was so beyond reproach that he, the accused, could essentially judge the accusers.

Murray himself sought to educate the board on the issue of tenure in the midst of the crisis:

> It is now generally recognized that freedom to think, to learn and to teach is vital to the life of the university. This academic freedom is at times interpreted to permit activities in speech and deed that make for a change in the form of the personnel of the Government of a university ...

> There is an insidious criticism that resorts to intrigue and insinuation and never comes into the open. Such criticism breeds an atmosphere of suspicion and jealousy, saps public confidence and ultimately weakens and paralyzes, if it does not destroy the institution which permits it to continue unchecked. Every man has the right to express his opinions of the administration of the institution in which he serves, but that carries with it corresponding responsibilities. He must be prepared to justify his criticism or take the consequences.[58]

While Murray suffered greatly from this crisis, his position as president was never more secure. The investigation uncovered no misappropriation of funds, and with the faculty clearly in Murray's favour, he continued as unquestioned head of the corporation. Never before, or afterwards, was the role of faculty members as employees clearer.

In 1938, shortly after Murray's retirement in 1937, Carlyle King, a junior professor in English, criticized current thinking as the world moved towards a second general war. "An outspoken pacifist and CCF activist, King made a series of speeches in 1938 and criticized British imperialism, attacked the policies of British Prime Minister Neville Chamberlain, and called for international disarmament."[59]

Some people publicly accused him of sedition, being a communist, and adversely influencing the minds of his students. In private meetings, the new president, James Thompson, told him to cease his public criticisms, which he did. The student newspaper, *The Sheaf*, published an article, "Does Academic Freedom Exist at This University?" and supported King's right to free speech. Clearly, there were obvious limits to freedom of speech on the faculty, which the administration determined.[60] Much like Barrow's managerial employees in "Twilight of the Idols," the administration regulated academic radicalism.[61] It did so in a private way, and in a manner of which the former president would approve.

Cultural Meaning: The "Wisconsin Idea" as Blueprint

The Wisconsin Idea, as Veysey suggests, brought about two major changes in American higher education. First, it introduced the expert into technical and social planning, thereby making academics much more influential. Second, it extended higher education directly to the people to provide classes to, and ultimately serve, the entire state.[62] This democratization elevated the service university to pre-eminence in American higher education, particularly in the Midwest. Vocational and professional schools expanded rapidly, especially in agriculture and engineering.

Before construction began at the University of Saskatchewan in 1910, policy makers had to decide what kind of institution it would become. As we saw at the outset of this chapter, Murray had declared it a people's university – one that would avoid the denominational struggles of its eastern Canadian counterparts while serving every corner of the province. In his first "Report of the President" in June 1908, he wrote, "In Wisconsin they [the governors who travelled south] saw an admirable example of a University whose watchword is service of the State. In the University of that State there is a happy blending of the best of the old and the new – a harmonious combination of the Liberal Arts and Pure Sciences with the Sciences applied to Agriculture and the Professions."[63] As a people's university serving the province, the new institution would have the study of agriculture at its core.

Central to its *meaning* to the people was the location of the College of Agriculture. In a province where the primary industry was farming, and where virtually every secondary industry somehow related to farming, its location would dictate if Saskatchewan would live up to the spirit of Murray's statements or cater largely to the societal elite like its eastern predecessors. From the outset, Murray knew what he wanted – the agriculture college as the centrepiece to his campus. His challenge, however, was to convince the board and the province that this was best for the university and the province it served.

While on his southern sojourn, he liked most what he discovered at the University of Wisconsin.[64] There, according to historian Michael Hayden, Murray found his model. He wrote to his long-time friend University of Toronto President Sir Robert Falconer in 1930: "Perhaps the greatest contribution from American sources is the larger conception of the purpose and scope of a State University – the conception of it as the scientific arm of the state for Research, for carrying the benefits of Science to all and sundry in the state, and for the supply of information to Legislative assemblies and their Executives. To Saskatchewan Wisconsin appeared in 1908 as an excellent example of this kind of University as contrasted with the Oxford type – a place for Liberal Culture and preparation for the Learned Professions."[65]

Murray cited as models for the unified campus, where all colleges coexisted without waste, jealousy, or bitterness, the universities of Wisconsin, Illinois, Minnesota, and Missouri; each was "strong, efficient and progressive."[66] The creation of a strong College of Agriculture as the centrepiece to his new university was a further reflection of his Wisconsin experience.[67] As he travelled throughout the American Midwest and Ontario and Manitoba, he asked many "university men" about how to convince his board to house a College of Agriculture on the campus, and only G.C. Creelman, president of the Ontario Agricultural College in Guelph, opposed uniting agriculture with the university's other work, but he gave no reason.[68] Presidents of Midwestern and northern Plains universities and even President Pritchett of the CFAT agreed that Agriculture should stand alongside the other branches of learning and on the same campus. Murray rejected Creelman's eastern-Canadian advice in favour of a Wisconsin, or Midwest model.

The Canadian-born president of Missouri, A. Ross Hill – a close friend and confidant – outlined his recommendations:

> 2. With reference to the location of the Agricultural College, by all means have that made a department of the University. In any case you will need to have a campus of reasonable size for your University, instead of locating the institution in the midst of a city or large town. If you locate the institution on the outskirts of a town you can easily have adjoining it the land necessary for an experimental farm, and it is entirely desirable that you have the whole University on one campus ... I have worked for eleven years in universities that included Colleges of Agriculture, and I see no serious disadvantages in the intimate relationship. You are able thereby to graduate a more cultured body of agricultural students, and you avoid duplication of fundamental sciences that will be necessary if you have the Agricultural College established as a distinct institution. The most difficult problem connected with having the Agricultural College a department of the University arises from the fact that it is more difficult to maintain high standards of admission to the Agricultural College and at the same time reach the people in the communities which it serves.[69]

Ross's in-state colleague Chancellor D.A. Houston of Washington University in St Louis agreed: "In my judgment it is a hideous mistake to separate the agricultural from the other university work, and to locate any educational institution in the country. Preferably I should locate it in the suburbs of the largest city at all conveniently situated."[70]

Murray carefully crafted a report to his board in early 1909: "President James of Illinois writes 'It would be a great advantage to the University to be located in or near a large city.' Chancellor Houston of Washington University writes 'It would be a hideous mistake to locate any education institution in the country.'

President Van Hise of Wisconsin believes that 'the best location for a University is in the town of moderate size.' 'If a University is located in too small a place it dominates the community, if in too large a city it is lost.' President Pritchett says 'It is impossible to conduct technical departments and professional schools in a small town.'"[71] Although Murray and his companions had travelled to Canada's east, and Murray had solicited advice from university men in Ontario, he made no mention of Ontario in his report. Wisconsin was his model.

Murray took the Wisconsin Idea a step further by pushing for the province's capital city to house its new university, just as Wisconsin and several other states had done in their capitals. In that location, Murray quotes his American brethren, the university better serves the entire jurisdiction, has more influence on legislation, and provides scientific advisers in all directions. "The greatest reason is the service the University can render the State. Wisconsin, we were told, renders its state three to five times more service than the Universities which are distant from their capitals. Last year Wisconsin had 41 professors serving the State in various capacities, some in three or four, and nearly all gratuitously."[72]

Although Murray envisioned the campus in Regina, his voice on the board was only one of nine. The decision resided with the governors, but provincial politics also played a role. The recent election had returned Conservatives to seats in both Moose Jaw and Prince Albert, so Liberal Premier Walter Scott disqualified those cities. The choice lay between Saskatoon and Regina. The vote occurred on 9 April 1909, but was never officially recorded, nor were the contents of the discussions disclosed. By a vote of either 5–4 or 6–3, Saskatoon was victorious.[73] Though unsuccessful in regard to location, Murray maintained the Wisconsin Idea as the central meaning to the new university. All commentators agree that taking learning, particularly in agricultural science, to all corners of the province has been Saskatchewan, and Murray's, greatest achievement.[74]

From the time the University of Saskatchewan was first imagined, the agricultural college was to be an integral part of the campus and the province. Arthur Morton confides that even though the college of arts and science would enrol the most students, everyone knew that agriculture would have pride of place.[75] Elsewhere in Canada, agricultural colleges sat away from the central campus and conducted research at arm's length from the university. Saskatchewan was the first Canadian university to house the college of agriculture on its campus, as Madison and other US universities did. Maintaining university control over agricultural and teacher training, argued Murray, was key to achieving a close relationship with the life of the province.[76]

Creating a diverse and active extension program would take science and technology to the people. The university created such a department in 1910. Its main focus was agricultural, even though most Saskatchewan farmers thought learning farming from professors somewhat laughable.[77] Regardless, from 1913–14 on, travelling professors encouraged "agricultural societies, plowing matches, homemakers clubs, winter meetings, seed grain fairs, stallion shows, and standing fields competitions and short courses."[78] The university made its building available to those keen to improve farming. A mobile library of technical books and fiction accompanied instructors in their travels. Lectures in philosophy and history also took place in some of the province's major cities. Although agricultural practice was the focus, Murray encouraged professors in many disciplines to take their service to the people.

The university's vocational focus is clear in the growth of professional schools from its founding until 1937.[79] Law in 1912 became the third independent college on campus. By 1913, the College of Pharmacy began work with one instructor. In 1914, what was to become the College of Business started offering a bachelor of accounting. Much as on US campuses, the approach of a world war, and its onset for Canada in 1914, greatly increased demand for skilled engineers and professionals with training in the practical sciences. In 1914, a School of Civil Engineering started up; by 1916, the College of Engineering was in operation, and during the 1920s it added classes in agricultural, ceramic, electrical, and mechanical engineering.[80] The School of Household Science began in 1928.[81] These developments in vocational education were part of a larger, continental movement towards greater *social efficiency*,[82] or, as Levine would argue, a North American *culture of aspiration*, that made higher education a route for addressing the social and economic expectations of society.[83] Similarly, Barrow's assertion that the American university became an ideological tool to create a corporate ideal to control the means of mental production also fits the Saskatchewan experience.[84] Whatever the reason for this *culture of emulation*, I believe that these US developments in society and higher education almost always antedate similar Canadian advances. Canadian higher education in this period was in a constant state of emulation, rather than of innovation.[85]

It is also clear from Murray's own statements that much of what he did in creating his university was a move away from Canadian models. "Nearly every University has suffered because short views were taken in the beginning. It is true that fifty years ago it was well-nigh impossible to forecast the extent of the growth of a progressive University. McGill, Toronto, Queen's, Dalhousie and Manitoba are notorious examples of overcrowding."[86] Murray commended the work of Presidents Angell of Michigan, Schurman of Cornell, and Judson of Chicago. Particularly in his early years at Saskatoon, but certainly throughout his tenure, it was American institutions to which he turned for inspiration, and eastern Canadian campuses from which he turned away.

When contemplating the meaning of what was then Saskatchewan's only university, one cannot help but think that Murray imposed its meaning from above. The institution, while certainly somewhat the people's university, is really Murray's, for he, more than any individual or law, dictated to whom the university would open its doors and, through his unilateral hiring practices, who would grace the halls of his campus as an employee. In assuring that Regina College could not rival it, he ensured his own place as the supreme expert of higher education in the province.

Pastoralism, as it has unfolded in history and in the United States, implies an idealization of the rural life, and Murray reified this vision in his university. By placing the College of Agriculture at its centre, and maintaining an Extensions Division reaching to every corner of the province, with agricultural practice at its core, he was guaranteeing the continuation of the idealized rural life in Saskatchewan. By keeping his as the only campus in the province, thereby guaranteeing his own pre-eminence in policy making, he ensured that the aesthetic, morally superior, and regenerating existence of country life in the province could continue. [87]

Historians of the west such as Richard Slotkin argue that such pastoral myths reduce the world to a series of compelling metaphors, in this case to motivate people to leave the east and head west. If, as Slotkin suggests, myths contain three basic elements – a hero, a universe in which the hero can act, and a narrative describing the hero's action – then certainly the history of Walter Murray's University of Saskatchewan is a myth that he himself created.[88]

Any history of the University of Saskatchewan, from its creation through the long tenure of its first president, must pay homage to those institutions, structures, and principles around which it grew – the state and land-grant universities of the American Midwest. Although the University of Saskatchewan was truly unique in Canada, it was very much a product of that first visit by Walter Murray and his board of governors to those "southern universities whose problems were similar to those of Saskatchewan." In unquestioningly transplanting an American corporate model onto the Canadian prairies, Murray made his institution part of a larger North American "club" of major state/provincial universities. By rationalizing organization, pursuing the Carnegie Foundation's influence and financial support, and regulating faculty dissent and academic freedom, not to mention the tacit acceptance of these structures by the university's faculty, Murray did achieve what the 1907 University Act intended – a world-class institution.

With Murray's departure in 1937, however, came the departure of Carnegie financial support. The American corporate model was firmly entrenched, yet Canadian corporations lacked the strength, sophistication, and financial resources to carry through on the promise of the American model. As US Midwest state universities found myriad ways to generate income and remain competitive in a ruthless North American market, the University of Saskatchewan continued to depend on government funding in a province whose revenue depends entirely on the vicissitudes of an agrarian economy with comparatively minuscule corporate or individual endowments. Regardless, the American notion of the *service* university remains a cornerstone to the institution's role and function. Although it now has a companion university in Regina, its taking of higher learning to all corners of the province, particularly in agriculture, remains its highest achievement. Even for this success alone, the Wisconsin Idea in higher education has served well the people and province of Saskatchewan.

◇◇◇◇◇◇◇

7

◇◇◇◇◇◇◇

Parallel Meanings:
Democracy and Education

WITHIN A CONTINENTAL PERSPECTIVE OF THE NORTH AMERICAN Great Plains, many policy makers, be they federal politicians in Ottawa, provincial cabinet ministers in Regina, university presidents in Saskatoon, or school inspectors in rural Saskatchewan, appropriated, purposefully, the symbols of the US west to make the Canadian west an extension of the American west, largely to entice migration and also to further development. The national government and its ministers of the interior – especially Laurier's, Clifford Sifton and Frank Oliver – borrowed or re-created these symbols, images, and meanings and assigned them to what would become the provinces of Alberta and Saskatchewan (see chapter 3, above).[1]

The unwitting result of this appropriation was a settlement that brought Americans and Europeans to an extension of the American west, where the prairie region's culture, institutions, and policies developed along longitudinal, not latitudinal, lines. These parallel developments in Saskatchewan maintained a close affinity with US Midwestern and Great Plains culture, institutions, and so on. This occurred often in resistance to, or rejection of, similar structures emanating from Canada's east, as was particularly obvious in Saskatchewan's K–12 schools and its sole university. The democratic *meaning* of education in the province was populist and Jeffersonian in origin between 1905 and 1937, and not that of the national Anglo-Celtic majority.

To claim that policy makers in Saskatchewan education adopted American language and social policy, to both articulate problems and propose solutions that were largely identical across the continental Plains, is perhaps not surprising. To historians such as Daniel T. Rodgers, who posits a North Atlantic social-policy community where policy alternatives moved freely throughout a region from Bogota to Berlin during a period of Progressive reform, such an argument is but a localized case study of a large-scale theory.[2] It is evidence of a transfer of social policy, but not necessarily of culture. If, however, the language of reform indicates the sharing of meanings, then this commonality suggests a much deeper and more profound transfer of culture. When US Midwestern and Plains culture moved northward to Saskatchewan, it took with it more than simply a language of reform. In the context of K–12 education, moralistic, populist political culture carried with it shared meanings of the rural schools and, because of problems with those institutions, meanings of their consolidation.

This chapter extends the arguments of chapters 4 and 5 regarding the meaning of rural schools and consolidation, but here within the context of populist and moralistic ideology. I begin with American meanings and then compare these to the reception of parallel meanings in Saskatchewan. Finally, I further characterize the University of Saskatchewan within this continental, populist Plains and Midwestern mentality.

RURAL SCHOOLS AND CONSOLIDATION

American Meanings

For American writers on the rural school such as Mabel Carney, Elwood Cubberly, and Harold Foght, consolidation of rural schools was about more than increasing efficiency – it represented nothing less than living up to the ideals of the US founding fathers. For this reason, their language of reform often assumed an almost evangelical, crusading tone. Foght's plea in 1910 was consistent: "Consolidation ... is a plan to reconstruct the rural schools on a new foundation which will re-establish the ancient principle of 'equal rights to all.'"[3] Equality of opportunity, the grounding concept of the American common school, was the goal. For Foght, however, that hope had long since died because the farm youth "has not had a square deal."[4]

Cubberly agreed wholeheartedly: "That the education provided for such children is what it ought to be, or might easily be made to be, few maintain. Rural children are entitled to something better, and the interests of the state demand that there be a better equalization of opportunities and advantages of education, as between the city boy or girl on the one hand and the boy and girl in the small villages and the rural districts on the other."[5] Cubberly saw an inherent city bias in the outmoded curriculum, which was central to the rural school problem: "The uniform textbooks, which have been introduced by law, were books written primarily for the city child; the graded course of study, which was superimposed from above, was a city course of study; the ideals of school became, in large part, city and professional in type ... The subjects of instruction have been formal and traditional, and the course of instruction has been designed more to prepare for entrance to a city or town high school than for life in the open country. So far as the school was vocational in spirit, it has been the city vocations and professions for which it has tended to prepare its pupils, and not the vocations of the farm and the home."[6]

For Foght, the banal life of the city (that place where rural school students would eventually head) itself was reason enough to improve rural schooling: "City life is terribly devitalizing. In its artificial, hot-house atmosphere the human organism literally starves and early deteriorates. Into this life, then, our best country boys and girls are thrown annually by the hundreds of thousands – their manifest destiny to reinforce the ebbing vitality of city life. The infusion of the sturdy country stock into the city assures a continuation of city prosperity and progress. But at what awful cost!"[7]

The goal of rural school consolidation was therefore to retain country life through municipal schools (schools in nearby, larger centres to which rural students travelled): "In order to re-establish this educational equality [equal rights for all] it becomes necessary to give the twelve million boys and girls living in the [US] rural communities just as thorough a preparation in school for their life work as we are now offering city children. Consolidation of rural schools is the practical remedy, and wherever given a fair trial it has provided conclusively that just as good, just as thorough-going schools may be made to flourish in the beneficent rural environment as in the city."[8] Consequently, rural schools were not solely about preparation for life in the country, or in town. Clearly, consolidating schools was crucial for the survival of rural communities and ultimately of country life in an increasingly industrial age.

Foght wrote in 1912: "Any form of education, to be effective, must reflect the daily life and interests of the community employing it. With us, agriculture is the chief primary industry; consequently our rural education must be agricultural in nature."[9] The American expert's clearest statement on the subject came while he was analysing Saskatchewan's schools in 1918: "To educate all its people, without exception, is both the duty and the right of democracy. There are in Saskatchewan thousands of adults classed as illiterates – a majority of them from foreign shores. If these people have been deprived of educational opportunities in their youth, it is the duty of the government to extend [that] blessing now in their years of maturity; if they have neglected their earlier opportunities, democracy has the right to demand that they correct the deficiency with government assistance at once. For all such people there should be established, as part of the regular school system, night schools, part time schools, and other types of continuation schools."[10]

Mabel Carney agreed with Foght: "A special function of the country school, imposed by present rural conditions, is that it shall become an initiator of various phases of rural progress and a center for the building of the community. The *complete function* of the country school may be summarized in the phrase, *the country school as a center for redirected education and community building.*"[11] She viewed the rural school as "a democratic community institution, representing the *whole* community."[12]

Writing some 60 years later, David Tyack captures the populist bent in the meaning of the American rural school, particularly as it existed in the west: "the center – educational, social, dramatic, political, and religious – of a pioneer community."[13] "As one of the few social institutions which rural people encountered daily, the common school both reflected and shaped a sense of community ... [It] integrated rather than disintegrated the community."[14]

Most important is Tyack's conception of who controlled it: "Most rural patrons had little doubt that the school was theirs to control and not the property of the professional educator."[15] Jonathan Raban echoes a similar populist characterization of the rural school in Montana: "The schoolhouse was an emblem of the fact that people were here for keeps. The foundations were dug deep enough into the prairie to hold one's ambitious roots. It was a showcase for everyone's best efforts at carpentry, painting, needlework, plumbing. And it was a political nursery. Forming a school district, electing a school board, dealing with county and state education agencies, the honyockers [Montana slang for 'homesteaders'] learned how to work the American system of do-it-yourself grassroots democratic government."[16] Given this meaning, it is little wonder that local patrons were loath to surrender their influence to the expert.

The rural school was the single democratic entity closest to the people, and consolidation threatened that local control. The issue of who was in charge confounded efforts at consolidation in both the rural American and Saskatchewan cultures. In the United States, in the interests of efficiency, the expert prevailed over the local patron, while in Saskatchewan the local patron carried the day despite the government's wishes and the efforts of experts such as Harold Foght.[17] Populist rhetoric, though powerful in the US Midwest and northern Plains, could not overcome the expert's influence. North of the border, in contrast, calls for efficiency, whether from the province or from a populist, administrative progressive from the American Plains, could not dispel the power of populism among the people.

Saskatchewan Meanings

Harold Foght took with him to Saskatchewan a decidedly populist language and found himself far from alone in his democratic utterances. As early as 1913, school inspectors were making similar pleas to fairness in regard to school consolidation. "The chief nation-builders of the province are the pioneers on the frontier. After all the hardship that they must endure, is it fair to penalize their children, condemning them to a meagre education, whilst the children of the city made great by their labour have every educational advantage?"[18] In 1914, another inspector wondered: "But in spite of improvements here and there, of various remedial measures that have been attempted and of the excellent financial basis of the system, the rural school still remains the unsolved problem, not of this province only, but of every other province of the Dominion and of nearly every state in the American Union. It does not accomplish the work it should and might in the interests of the province as a whole. As compared with the city or town school its efficiency is low. This is regrettable both from the point of view of the state and that of the rural school child. Has the rural school child the right to ask the state to furnish him with educational facilities equal to those provided for the urban child?"[19]

In presenting his *Survey* on Saskatchewan schools, Foght was "preaching to the converted" in Regina and among school inspectors. "If now the artificial lines separating these [local] districts were removed, and all the wealth of the municipality were equalized for educational uses every boy and girl would have reason to expect equalized educational opportunity in uniformly strong well-paid teachers, long terms, well-maintained school buildings, and well-sustained school work."[20] In consolidation, "the municipality becomes the unit of taxation for educational purposes, thus guaranteeing equality of educational opportunity to all living within the community."[21] He intended uniform and universal application of his recommendations.

◇◇◇

Just as Carney identified the rural school as a social centre for the community, so too did policy makers in Saskatchewan: "One finds considerable satisfaction in the increasing evidence that the people are awakening to the recognition of the fact the school is the centre of the community. With the recognition of this fact will come the beginning of the solution of ruralising or socializing of the rural school."[22] In 1912, one inspector spoke in decidedly populist terms: "One is almost ashamed to admit that in the great majority of districts the school is below the general standard of the community. The people as a whole do not realize how deeply children are impressed by the natural world around them. The school should be the centre of the community; this centre should be attractive and powerful in influence. It is the most tremendously significant thing in the whole history of America. Here is gathered the most impressionable element, to secure the highest possible development of mind and character. Every element of order, neatness and beauty, every broadening influence, every appeal to the finer nature of the child, mean[s] better men and women and a more thrifty, prosperous, and attractive community."[23]

By 1915, the government created Rural Education Associations to promote the school as the centre for every community. "The object of these associations will be to promote and develop the use of school gardens as an educational factor, to organize school fairs, contests for boys and girls, boys' and girls' clubs, etc., to organize literary societies and to encourage the use of the school building as a community centre; in fact, an attempt will be made to make these associations feel responsible for the general educational advancement of the whole community."[24]

School gardens were a very successful enterprise across rural Saskatchewan, as they were across the United States and parts of Europe, and went far in enabling rural schools to prepare rural youth for life on the farm. By the late 1920s, however, they were slowly disappearing, and with the onset of drought in 1930 they disappeared completely.

Closely akin to Foght, Saskatchewan inspectors observed: "The efficiency of your schools is not to be measured by the number of students who pass their examinations but by the provision that is made for the education of every child in the district and the solid foundation laid for future citizenship. We must keep in mind the fact that the great majority of our pupils are not going in the High Schools but into actual business of some kind or other; we should then prepare them for the life they must live so that they may be intelligent and useful citizens."[25] As for who should control the rural school, inspectors reiterated Tyack's argument about rural schools in the American west: "It is therefore evident that the development of our rural schools cannot be more rapid than will be the evolution of the people who administer its affairs. This evolution can be done only by the extension of the knowledge of the meaning and needs of the school as an institution which is directly under the control of the people for whom it has been created and established."[26] Finally, in the spirit of Raban, John Charyk denotes the same meaning to the rural school in Saskatchewan as did Raban in Montana. "The country schoolhouse was a proud moment in the building of this nation. It represented the heart and soul of every rural district and was the centre around which the religious, political, social, and educational life of the community revolved."[27]

Educational policy makers in Saskatchewan in the 1910s shared with their American cousins – people such as Carney, Cubberly, and Foght – the same meaning of the rural school problem and its solution. They also agreed on the populist meaning of consolidation and of the rural school itself. At the level of the local patron – in populist lingo, the people – each polity ascribed identical meanings to the local school and believed that it, not the expert, was in control. According to Tyack, about 1910, control over US local schools began transferring from the people to the experts.[28] To put it another way, populism gave way to the work of the professional educators such as Foght. Even though many policy makers thought of Foght as the one expert who could perhaps trigger school consolidation, Saskatchewan would not follow suit until the 1940s.

Regardless of the enthusiasm preceding Foght and his work, and the fervour that followed its completion, by 1922 the effort had virtually stopped. Foght had also recommended appointment of a special inspector to reorganize schools after consolidation. In his 1927 annual report, this official laid to rest any plans for consolidation: "The present method, of administering school districts by boards of trustees elected by ratepayers in each district is the result of long practice and almost without exception proves very satisfactory. There seems no general desire to change in this regard, although one occasionally hears of the advantages to be derived from a larger unit of administration. It must be said that on the whole the trustees are an earnest and efficient body of men."[29] Furthermore, by 1924, Rural Education Associations were in a state of decline across the province.[30]

Interesting, however, the notion of school consolidation and centralization persisted within at least one urban school division. In June 1927, Superintendent Dr Snell told the board of trustees of the Saskatoon School District that his chief concern was for the 20 centres in the province that retained two or more boards of education. However, he also revealed a populist perspective in his recommendations: "2. replace the individual School Boards in rural districts by a Board of Education for the municipality, or small group of municipalities, to provide school facilities where needed and of such a character as will enable rural boys and girls to obtain their elementary and secondary education under those conditions that will not entice them away from rural life, and that will not sever home connections during a critical period in their lives; 3. foster the introduction of a course of study better suited to the aptitude of the individual pupil."[31] Snells's statement bears striking resemblance to similar ones by Foght[32] and, like so many pronouncements from the province's administrative elite, had virtually no effect.

Although consolidation of American rural schools met resistance in a variety of locales, the process was under way in virtually all states by the time Foght arrived in Saskatchewan. In fact, consolidation successes in North Dakota and Minnesota informed Foght's recommendations north of the border. Whereas US consolidation or centralization of rural schools was a success, it was

an abject failure in Saskatchewan until the 1940s. This single failure challenges my argument that Saskatchewan's policy makers
looked south to solve prairie Canadian problems: if this were true,
a province intent on resisting eastern Canadian models of reform
would have gratefully welcomed consolidation, as it did so many
other shared solutions to common problems.

Consolidation's failure in Saskatchewan is not a reflection of
Foght's inability to convince the province's bureaucratic elite to
accept American solutions to largely identical problems. Foght's
recommendations were well received by school inspectors and
provincial government employees alike. Instead, its failure confirms that local control of democratic entities – a cornerstone of
American democracy and populist revolt – had migrated northward and dug deeper roots in prairie Canadian soil than in the
United States. Local control had first taken seed in the early
United States, and later germinated in the soil of the American
Midwest and Plains, but it bore its greatest fruit not there, but
through its transplantation into the fields of Saskatchewan. The
locals' resistance to school consolidation suggests a far deeper reception of this aspect of American culture than they displayed
vis-à-vis US-style centralization of schools. People felt this most
acutely in their intimate relationship with that level of democratic
government closest to them – the local school board.

The Failure of Consolidation

Contemporary writers on rural school consolidation on either side of
the forty-ninth parallel commented that it allowed retention of bet-
ter-qualified teachers, equalized taxation and opportunity, encouraged better attendance, proved more efficient and cost-effective,
and in general provided better education for all students.[33] While
this was certainly the case in the American context, some arguments
were not true in Saskatchewan. Conveyance, for example, was much
more expensive there than in the American Midwestern and Plains
states. This was the case for several reasons, including the greater
distances within the municipality, poorer roads, and the length
and ferocity of the Saskatchewan winter. While Frederick Jackson

Turner proclaimed, rather prematurely, the end to the American frontier at the close of the nineteenth century, frontier conditions persisted on the Canadian prairies well into the 1920s.

Even though Saskatchewan in 1914 legislated subsidies to local school districts covering up to one third of the cost of travel to school via horse-drawn buses, school boards still had to pay the remainder. In many rural school districts, particularly where sparse settlement limited the tax base, the cost was prohibitive.[34] Furthermore, Funk argues, the act providing subsidies for students to travel to another, centralized municipal district in fact kept local school districts afloat, even if they had no operating schools.[35] The legislation increased the number of school districts in the province.

Patterns of settlement also impeded consolidation. As we saw in chapter 3, many immigrants, like pioneers on the American frontier, created communities as fragments of the home country, settling with people like themselves, often even from the same district.[36] Despite ties of kinship, religion, and other attributes, the geographical locations were often quite random. A homogeneous settlement of German Lutherans might be just a few miles from a cohesive group of Orthodox Ukrainians. In the US Midwest, these contiguous communities had by 1918 (when rural school consolidation was in full swing there) coexisted for a generation and had built links with each other through commerce, other forms of contact, and Americanization, partly by public schooling. This made consolidation far easier there about 1900 than it would be in Saskatchewan in 1918, when settlement was far from complete and the local school had not accomplished much homogenizing. Local control in the northern US Plains had reached its apex decades earlier, but in the early twentieth century was on the wane.

Much of my hypothesis in chapters 3 and 4 rejects a macro-level approach to Canadian political culture and education policy, and I reluctantly invoke here a national perspective. Scholars such as Tyack and Lipset identify a late-nineteenth-century US national movement towards centralization,[37] but in the 1920s and 1930s in Canada the reverse process was in full swing. Canadian political scientist Garth Stevenson finds *centrifugal* federalism in operation from Confederation until the 1930s, whereby power that once resided within the central government in Ottawa devolved to the provinces. This decentralization occurred as the United States centralized through *centripetal* forces.[38] In this regard, American efforts at consolidation reflect a more general national trend, just as Saskatchewan's resistance to centralization was itself part of an opposite trend in Canada, particularly in Saskatchewan, whose population, more than that of any other province, remained over-whelmingly rural.

US schooling centralized during a period of urbanization and industrialization that began in the later nineteenth century. Although there were a few American states as rural as Saskatchewan, schools consolidated in urban and rural states alike.[39] One must assume that in 1918 Harold Foght anticipated a similar urbanizing trend in Saskatchewan. "North America, it is shown, has long ago passed through its period of pioneering; the middle stage of exploitation and wastefulness of natural resources is now beginning to yield to organised, efficient, industrial life; but the schools, it is argued, have been slow to respond to changing national life."[40] In 1911, 73 per cent of Saskatchewan's population was rural; in 1921, 70 per cent was, and in 1931, 68 per cent. In 1941, the figure was lower still, at 67 per cent, but by 1951, it was back at 70 per cent.[41] From 1905 until well into the 1960s, the majority of residents was neither urban nor industrialized, but rural and agrarian.

As the rest of Canada and the United States urbanized throughout the first half of the twentieth century, settlement patterns in Saskatchewan between 1910 and 1960 remained consistent. For every one resident who settled in an urban community, two established roots in the country. The growth of school divisions reflects this demographic reality over the same period. About the time of Foght's survey in 1917, the number of school divisions in the province exceeded four thousand; a decade later, there were over five thousand, each boasting its own school board with three trustees.[42]

The above facts help explain why attempts at consolidating rural schools failed in the 1920s and 1930s. Tyack's argument in *The One Best System* shows that reform of the American rural school revealed a successful transfer of power from the layman to the professional.[43] Indeed, Progressive attempts at reforms throughout

American social policy, including public education, health, and alcohol consumption, increased centralization and popular acceptance of expert control. In Saskatchewan, experts such as school inspectors and policy wonks in the provincial bureaucracy thought highly of Foght's recommendations and eagerly anticipated their implementation following 1918. Among the people, however, and representatives they elected from their communities, the same level of approval never developed. Resistance was not dismissal of American-style reform *per se*, but showed ironically that the people of Saskatchewan had adopted a democratic conception that was Jeffersonian, populist, and moralistic in tone. In Saskatchewan, inaction on Foght's call to consolidate rural schools exemplified a victory of the people over the expert.

Among the few histories of Saskatchewan's system of K–12 schooling, all commentators agree that, logistical issues aside, the failure of rural school consolidation in the 1920s came from the desire to preserve local control over local schools. In 1971, Funk asserted: "The Municipal School Movement [to consolidate rural schools] was a threat to the local board's sovereignty. It is the author's contention that this authority was more important than a good school in many instances."[44] University of Saskatchewan historian of education M.P. Scharf concurs: "There were a number of reasons for this. The state of the roads in the pioneer rural areas, the difficulties of winter travel, the scarcity of population, and the costs of conveyance were major operational factors inhibiting the acceptance of larger jurisdictions. However, even in the areas that had been settled for two generations and possessed better roads, another factor arose: local pride. One amalgamation arrangement, under which one school district ceased to exist, failed to recognize the local loyalty and identity that had already grown up in the local school districts. The fear of school closures cemented widespread resistance to school district restructuring."[45]

Yet, even though the results of Foght's *Survey* failed to live up to the high expectations, its recommendations did guide the debate for decades. I asserted above that explicit within calls for rural school consolidation by experts such as Elwood Cubberly and Harold Foght, and for the resolution to the "rural school problem" both in the United States and Saskatchewan, was a populist notion of equality of opportunity for all students, including disadvantaged rural residents. Equally powerful, but somewhat paradoxical to calls for improved rural schooling, are the Jeffersonian and populist calls to maintain local control over local schools. While Americans did not invent local control, they greatly furthered its practical application. This democratic conception migrated northward to Saskatchewan, integral to the larger cultural framework that I outlined above in chapter 3. The rejection of Foght's recommendations on consolidation was much less a spurning of American solutions for identical Saskatchewan problems than it indicated widespread acceptance of American democratic meanings and practice into the Canadian prairies.

Long-time University of Saskatchewan professor of political science John C. Courtney captures the unique relationship between Canadian federalism and American conceptions of local control.

The American conception of democracy has developed on the theory that in order to be truly democratic a political system must be "as close to the people as possible." I think it is not unfair to say that this concept of closeness is in the mainstream of American democracy from Jefferson through to the *Saturday Evening Post* ... This way of thinking of democracy has affected Canada most significantly. Not only has the nineteenth-century English liberal conception of local control been instrumental in the adoption and retention of "localized" education in Canada, but the peculiar conception of democracy, when combined with the institution of federalism in Canada, has added some considerable weight to the arguments of those who desire the continuance of local control. The combination of the English Fabians, John S. Mill, *The Federalist Papers*, and Jacksonian ideals presents a formidable opposition to those who favour a centralized system of educational control.[46]

In Saskatchewan, American derivatives of local control would be far more influential than their British equivalents. In this already-fertile environment for local control a plethora of farmer's movements and other forms of member organizations strengthened the impetus.

◇◇◇

When Seymour Martin Lipset's comprehensive study of Saskatchewan political culture, *Agrarian Socialism*, appeared in the late 1940s, the province had consolidated most of its rural schools, after the election of the Co-operative Commonwealth Federation in 1944. Recalling his own study some 20 years later, Lipset noted the remarkable degree of local participation among Saskatchewan's farmers:

> Each small rural community required some people to serve on the school board, on the local Wheat Pool Committee, on the board of the Cooperative Store, in the local telephone company, in the hospital, in the library, as Rural Municipality councillors, and so on. A total of at least 125,000 positions had to be filled by a few hundred thousand farmers. Many of course held three or four positions. I estimated that one out of eight farmers held a community post. And this meant, of course, that those who did not were in close personal contact with those who did, could receive information from those involved with problems and changes, and could tell them what they wanted done. Consequently, rural Saskatchewan was an organized community with considerable involvement in local institutions. People participated, not because they were convinced of the worth of the participation as an abstract principle but, rather, because the very existence of the community required a high degree of activity.[47]

Lipset concluded that such a high level of direct political involvement, within the institutions that most affected residents' lives, was positively Jeffersonian. However, despite more than five thousand school boards, rural students received poorer education than their urban cousins.[48] Regardless, Lipset, Courtney, and Funk all agree that an ideology for local control persisted in Saskatchewan well into the 1930s – far longer than in the American polity.

When one further considers Saskatchewan's *moralistic* political culture in the early twentieth century, it becomes even more obvious why voters expected to control their local schools. Elazar reminds us that within this subculture – with its epicentre in the Midwest and Plains states, the source of most American settlers to Saskatchewan – political involvement was central to life in the commonwealth. "Since the moralistic political culture rests on the fundamental conception that politics exists primarily as a means to coming to grips with the issues and public concerns of civil society, it also embraces the notion that politics is a concern for every citizen, not just those who are professionally committed to political careers. Indeed, it is the duty of every citizen to participate in the political affairs of his commonwealth."[49]

Elazar adds that a moralistic political culture encourages greater acceptance of local-government intervention. "A willingness to encourage local government intervention to set public standards does not necessarily reflect a concomitant willingness to allow outside governments equal opportunity to intervene."[50] This framework helps us grasp why Saskatchewan's people rejected provincial attempts at consolidation and defended their control over local schools against outsiders.

The fact that different elements perceived and received Midwest and Plains culture in competing ways is not surprising. As William H. Sewell, Jr, reminds us, cultures are inherently contradictory. He notes, for example, Christian symbolism (and theology) unify in one figure "three sharply distinct and largely incompatible possibilities of Christian religious experience: authoritative and hierarchical orthodoxy (the Father), loving egalitarianism and grace (the Son), and ecstatic spontaneity (the Holy Ghost)."[51] Within populism, the rural school came to mean entirely different things to administrative progressives and to the people. For the bureaucrat, it impeded change and equality of opportunity. For the local patron, however, it remained the democratic focus for community life and popular control. The survival of it, and its board, meant the preservation of rural life, not its demise. In the American context, local control gave way to centralization. In Saskatchewan K–12 schooling, at least from 1918 through 1930, the local patron prevailed over the expert.

At the University of Saskatchewan, American Midwestern and Plains meanings of higher education evolved at a time when the institution's first president, Walter Murray, pursued a corporate ideal, albeit under the guise of a "people's university." If, as Kevin Brooks suggests, the historian examines higher education in North America in continental and regional terms, rather than in a strictly national context, such an evolution appears inevitable, since universities in Canada's west developed to provide a general education, following American models, rather than the liberal education centring on the oratorical tradition of the British university in Canada's east.[52] Though somewhat dictatorial in his practice, Murray performed his duties as he and many of his colleagues saw fit. In doing so, he was most certainly a product of his time. Brooks sees Murray as an outgrowth of his eastern and Scottish educational roots. In my mind, however, his experience at Dalhousie and the University of Edinburgh served as negative examples for him in Saskatoon. Even though his practice as president falls short of a populist or democratic habit, the practice of his university, particularly through the work of the College of Agriculture, strikingly resembles populist reforms in US higher education.

Recent histories of American populism stress the Progressive influence on agrarian reform efforts. Charles Postel, for example, posits that US farm reformers pinned much of their hope for rural renewal on scientific education, even though they disagreed with professors on what to teach. Farmers, he argues, tended to resent the intellectuals' emphasis on laboratory science, favouring a business approach to farming. Correspondingly, the intellectuals viewed the farmer as indifferent to science. Regardless, each side sought salvation through science and wanted higher education to span the rural–urban divide.[53] Americans set up programs in agricultural and mechanical arts at institutions such as Iowa State College, North Carolina State University, and the University of Wisconsin. The Saskatchewan campus mirrored those developments to a remarkable degree.

In choosing agriculture as the centrepiece to his university, President Murray obviously grasped its role for a province that remained, well into the mid-twentieth century, rural and agrarian, and his early statements committed the new institution to the service of the people. Although he did not say so, such actions intended to maintain the vitality of the countryside. The study of agriculture would not lure rural residents to the city, as might be the case in an institution devoted to liberal arts, but instead prepare them to flourish on the farm. Agriculture would not serve the university, but vice versa.

Similarly, the Extensions Division would take science to every corner of the province. In so doing, Murray's words, and the deeds of his university, emulated those of the University of Wisconsin and its president, Charles Van Hise, who, in 1904 articulated the "Wisconsin Idea": "I shall never be content until the beneficent influence of the University reaches every home in the state."[54] Murray wanted the new university in Regina (like Van Hise's in Madison) so that it could more readily extend its influence into all facets of provincial life, including policy and research.

In rejecting the traditional eastern models, Murray adhered slavishly to the advice of his southern colleagues, such as Hill of Missouri. He took Hill's advice to choose instructors for his vocational colleges in Saskatoon from among graduates of land-grant and vocational universities such as Iowa State College. The hiring, retention, and success of hirees such as agricultural engineer Evan Hardy established this vocational emphasis in Saskatoon. Like the US colleges and universities that democratized American higher education, these colleges opened up Saskatchewan. When professors took sabbatical leave or sociological tours, they tended to visit the same land-grant and vocational institutions. These offered extra training and became rich sites for cultural transfer.

PARALLEL MEANINGS IN K-12 AND HIGHER EDUCATION

If one searches for parallel meanings between the province's K–12 school system and higher education in this era (something rare in the historiography of Saskatchewan education), commonalities emerge. Just as in K–12 schooling, centrifugal federalism affected higher education. As was the US case, so in Canada the Carnegie Foundation for the Advancement of Teaching (CFAT) and the Rockefeller Foundation assumed towering influence in a system devoid of national authority or standardization. The government in Ottawa, apart from providing some funding, left higher education largely to the provinces, which let institutions chart their own course. In the hands of a powerful and independent president such as Walter Murray, the University of Saskatchewan developed completely without governmental influence or political interference. Murray relished this autonomy and crafted an institution almost entirely by his own hand. In the process, however, he imposed corporate-like form and function.

At the level of the expert, while Foght was making his case to consolidate rural schools, thereby enabling the rural dweller to stay in the countryside, Murray had already crafted a program of study in Saskatoon to ensure precisely that outcome. In K–12 schooling, the "imaginary" divide between town and country – so prevalent in American populist rhetoric – made it difficult for rural farmers to surrender their young people to a consolidated town or municipal school. This reluctance grew more acute when the rural school remained the one site of local control for a group feeling control over little else. Surrendering the power to elect trustees, hire a teacher, build a school, and so on to an adjacent town was almost inconceivable to local residents.

Whereas Foght failed to bridge this divide between town and country, Murray succeeded. Initially, Saskatchewan farmers were every bit as reluctant to listen to the academics from his Extensions Division as they were to abide Foght's recommendation. Murray and his university succeeded, however, through long contact with people in all corners of the province – something Foght could not hope to accomplish.[55] Furthermore, with the work of Extensions, farmers could meet the intellectuals on their own terms, on home ground. Finally, Extensions sought to increase productivity on the farm, rather than reduce it, as many feared consolidation would do. Regardless, Harold Foght and Walter Murray agreed on the primacy of vocational, especially agricultural, education for Saskatchewan.

School inspectors such as Kennedy in Weyburn, in the south-eastern corner of the province, agreed. In 1916, he wrote to Dean of Agriculture Rutherford imploring the university to create a "Municipal Agricultural School" to better meet the needs for those students aged from 14 to 19 who planned to leave school after grade 8 – 94 per cent of people that age in the province, Kennedy estimated.[56] He couched his request in a language that spoke of the democratic purpose of schooling, writing to a dean who recognized that higher education must be relevant to the people – the two thought in the same populist, democratic language. However, Rutherford's marginal notes reveal his confusion – their different systems of education, one K–12, the other higher education, left them unable to communicate. There is no evidence of a response by him to Kennedy's request. The College of Agriculture did hold agricultural institutes throughout the province, but never created Kennedy's vision.

Historians of both K–12 and higher education in Saskatchewan highlight the anti-eastern perspectives. In 1918, Foght described the province's people as progressive of mind who avoided the back-east conservatism so prevalent elsewhere. Similarly, F.W.G. Haultain, the principal creator (as territorial premier) of the University of Saskatchewan, possessed, according to university historian Arthur S. Morton, a mind so virile that he could not follow slavishly the examples of eastern Canada. The rejection of eastern models of schooling was a persistent theme throughout the first four decades of the twentieth century.

In the turning away from the east, there must follow a turn towards somewhere else. For educators in Saskatchewan 1905–37, that turn was southward – inevitably taking them in the one direction that shared a common experience – an experience sewn in the dry and unforgiving soil of the US Midwest and Great Plains.

◇◇◇◇◇◇◇

8

◇◇◇◇◇◇◇

Putting It Together

EVENTS SINCE 1937

IN SPRING 1930, THE CHAIR OF THE SCHOOL MANAGEMENT
Committee for the Saskatoon School District, Dr Swanson, made
the following motion: "That it be laid down as a policy of this
Board that the Superintendent at least once in two years and
annually if possible, be instructed to proceed to those centres
where progressive educational policies are in operation, with a
view to seeking information that will be helpful in developing
the educational programme of this Board in all its phases ... That
the Superintendent be asked to begin with Easter Week 1930 to
proceed to certain centres of progressive education with a view to
carrying out the above policy."[1] The motion carried.

Such a clear statement is emblematic of the warm reception
for American-style Progressive education in Saskatchewan by
1930. Swanson certainly knew that "progressive centres" were
such US locales as Winnetka, Illinois. The ease with which
cultural practices, meanings, and language moved freely across
the continental Plains between about 1900 and 1930 leads one to
expect that such a process might continue unabated in ensuing
decades. This was not always the case.

The 1930s proved deeply trying for Saskatchewan and its
schools. The onslaught of the Depression and the "Dirty Thirties"

challenged rural life across the continent as the rural school problem quickly gave way to issues of survival generally. Alberta began
to consolidate rural schools in 1933 at the urging of communities
themselves, as the small rural district no longer was adequate.
Conversely, in Saskatchewan the desire for change persisted
from outside the local community, this time through the efforts
of teachers, who in 1933 created the Saskatchewan Teachers'
Federation. At the level of the people and their representatives,
the Saskatchewan School Trustees' Association, resistance to
consolidation persisted for the same reason as always: the fear
of losing local control over local schools. In Saskatchewan, the
people prevailed over the experts, albeit a different group of
experts, through the 1930s and 1940s.

Historian of education Michael Owen identifies three reasons
why teachers favoured consolidation: cost efficiency, improving
experiences for students, and self-interest.[2] They knew local
resistance well but attempted to reassure their neighbours that
reform need not compromise democratic local control. Moreover,
in emphasizing equity for students and efficiency in services,
they echoed the previous generation of populist experts such as
Foght. While one historian calls the nascent Teacher's Federation
"grassroots" because of its democratic structure, the grass beneath
its feet differed from that deep-rooted sward growing under farmers
for generations.[3] From the mid-1930s to the mid-1940s, rural
residents displayed far firmer roots than a fledgling professional
organization of teachers.

The 1940s also witnessed the advent of comprehensive collegiates in the province once the new Co-operative Commonwealth
Federation government extended vocationalism and pushed the
democratic purpose of schooling beyond the agricultural. While
some eastern Canadian historians view the comprehensive high
school as a colonial export from Britain to Canada,[4] Saskatchewan
imported it probably from US social-efficiency experts or administrative progressives. These developments swept American education during the First World War and accelerated with US entry
into the Second World War in late 1941.[5] By then vocationalism's
influence extended beyond the high school.

At the University of Saskatchewan, Walter Murray presided over the creation of vocational colleges of Business, Engineering, Household Science, and Pharmacy through the 1910s and 1920s, and retired in 1937. Beginning in autumn 1939, all the institutions of higher learning in Canada worked to support the war effort. When peace came, the federal Veteran's Rehabilitation Act (VRA) of 1945 ushered in a second wave of democratization in higher education by increasing access through federal funding of tuition for returning veterans. Like the famous US "GI Bill," it poured tens of thousands of men onto campuses all over the country.

Some institutions in both countries still received endowments from wealthy patrons and philanthropists, but creation in 1957 of the Canada Council lessened their influence in this country. Thereafter the federal government kept expanding its role in higher education.[6]

What has not changed at the University of Saskatchewan from its outset is perhaps most telling. Agriculture remains central – witness the new home (1991) for the College of Agriculture. Premier Grant Devine, an alumnus, championed the building, which stands out for its grand size and cost. Its architecture strays, like others of its era, from the campus's traditional Collegiate Gothic, but Health Sciences (2013) returns to Murray's architectural heritage.

More important, however, the central *meaning* of the university to the province remains intact. Following the central tenet of the Wisconsin Idea, this people's university still reaches out to every corner of the province. While it historically places a consistent third relative to neighbouring campuses at Manitoba and Alberta, and has yet to rival Oxford or Cambridge, as Laurier suggested it might, it remains the first choice for most Saskatchewan students in a "college marketplace" now continental in scope. In other words, its *meaning* to the people of Saskatchewan has stood constant.

As for K–12 education, history seems to repeat itself. Whereas it used to lag some 20 years behind new US *practices*, now developments arrive much sooner. Efforts at consolidation (now "rural division amalgamation") over the past decade have met resistance for the same old reason – local fear of losing control. Cost of conveyance and time on school buses remain problems. Now, with about

30 school divisions in the province, some the size of Prince Edward Island, the rural school problem has returned. The question today is far more dire: can the rural community survive without a rural school?

Similarly, the challenge of educating "new Canadians" is re-emerging as Saskatchewan experiences the strongest economic boom in the country. Foreign immigration has risen to the levels of the early twentieth century. Perhaps finally, almost a century later, the province is indeed the "last best west."

Furthermore, one may ask whether North Dakota's new "oil boom" will re-awaken interest in a north–south continental Plains culture, and ideally the telling of its history, as citizens around Minot repeat the experience of the Canadian oil patch. If "something in the soil" linked meaning and practice in a continental Plains culture a century ago, perhaps "something under the soil" can do the same, this time from north to south.[7]

Regardless, in writing a history of education in Saskatchewan, I do hope this volume might renew interest in a field too often dormant or untended. Historians need not wait for a centennial year to write about a topic (in this case, schooling) so central to understanding a province's cultural foundation(s). For if public schools and public universities attempt to replicate in their students what a polity deems most important within its people, if schools offer truly a "window into the soul" of a culture, then much "virgin" soil in historical analysis lies beyond the years of this study. One wonders, for example, what sorts of education policy emerged from diverging political cultures, as in Alberta's Social Credit (conservative) and Saskatchewan's Co-operative Commonwealth Federation (social-democratic) governments. Following the Second World War, what American cultural influences persisted within Saskatchewan education? Are the Saskatchewan Party's current educational policies a sign of eroding democratic ideals, or of their flowering? What can we learn from history about the returning rural school problem, or the resurfacing challenges in educating "new Canadians?"

And what of the *meaning* of Canada's west relative to its east? While politicians in the region west of Ontario flirted with western alienation and separatism, such views never really bore fruit at the level of the people. One might argue again that Quebec separatist movements in Canada's east – part of those related denominational squabbles that led people such as Walter Murray to head west – showed the west the model it most wanted to resist, or turn from.

ON MYTHS AND FRONTIERS

In my Introduction, I identified my *continentalist* perspective, which relies heavily on the early work of American scholars such as historian Paul Sharp and political sociologist Seymour Martin Lipset. In the spirit of this perspective, I indicated my desire to seek similarity rather than difference. I wish to return to the continental west here, but in a way that pays homage to some recent scholarship from both countries' historians in *comparative* history. Within the past decade, an outstanding two-volume study has examined the concept of the west(s) and the accompanying mythologies. I refer, of course, to Higham and Thacker's *One West, Two Myths*.[8] Much of their emphasis revolves around the two separate mythologies of the west that emerged on either side of the border: Frederick Jackson Turner's frontier thesis on US westward progress and Harold Innis and others' Laurentian thesis about Canada.

For those who write within the frontier thesis, the American west assumes a purifying myth that leaves the old world behind in the east. It becomes the site of progress to the point where, for American historian Richard White, the United States becomes the west writ large – so writes Canadian historian R. Douglas Francis.[9] In Canadian history, Francis asserts, progressive development occurs not in the west, nor in the hinterland, but in the metropolis back east along the St Lawrence. William H. Katerberg (a Canadian-trained historian practising on an American college campus) concurs, suggesting that in the United States the new – the frontier – made the country exceptional, whereas in Canada the old world of the east continued to dominate the west.[10] American Donald Worster, however, challenges such a perspective, suggesting instead that the settlement experience in Canada's west pushed away the old, traditional world of Canada's east.[11] These divergent national perspectives expose an intriguing lesson about looking at the mythology of the wests, American or Canadian. We each, Canadians and Americans, are academic spawn of our own respective myths. Perhaps it takes a "border-crossing" other, applying a foreign myth, to bring to light a process that otherwise might not be visible.

Take, for example, the occasion when Harold Foght first travelled to Saskatchewan in 1916. Turner's frontier thesis dominated American historiography. One could argue that Foght enunciated a frontier thesis when he spoke of Saskatchewanians as progressive-minded folks who sought to avoid the "back-eastern" conservatism of Ontario and the Maritimes. For him, and others who followed, such as Sharp, the Canadian west was a site of progress and not a replication of the old world. The Laurentian thesis was yet to unfold among the ranks of Canadian historians and would not penetrate American academic circles for quite some time.[12] It was Sharp who noted the similarities between the experience of the prairie Canadian farmer and his US Plains cousin, confirming that populists and Progressives alike created themselves in opposition to the east – home to the "interests" or plutocracy.

Sharp's first look into the Prairie west, *The Agrarian Revolt*, evoked the same frontier thesis in far clearer terms. As he noted in his Foreword: "American historians have often forgotten that the agricultural frontier lingered on in western Canada after it had disappeared in the United States. Thus the influence of a frontier region on American agriculture continued for many years after the American frontier had officially passed away. The forty-ninth parallel has been a far more formidable barrier to many historians than to the men and institutions they have examined."[13]

As I made the point in chapter 1, Sharp and Lipset were "right" the first time. For them, the strange was not yet familiar. Each arrived in Canada carrying his own American interpretation with him. As a historian, Sharp had already embraced the frontier thesis. For him, the frontier development of the Canadian prairies in the first half of the twentieth century mirrored the frontier American experience. As the Canadian west became more familiar to each scholar, however, their arguments changed. Lipset, on completion of his doctorate, assumed a teaching post at the

University of Toronto. While there, I suspect, he came to embrace a different mythology from the continental one in *Agrarian Socialism*, seeing difference rather than commonality.

I do not mean to suggest that Turner's frontier thesis should supplant the Laurentian as the prevailing myth of Canadian development in the west. What I do mean to suggest, however, is that a look southward for inspiration can often yield a different story from the typical. In my case, my extended passage on American interstates through the US heartland and Plains most certainly influenced my thinking about my home province of Saskatchewan and about western Canada. I am inextricably a product of my own "border-crossing" experiences – experiences not replicable in a reverse direction, or, I suppose, in any other direction for that matter. Robert Thacker reflects one certain outcome of my seemingly unusual path through academe in his introduction to volume II of *One West, Two Myths,* where he argues that understanding the Canadian west requires reference to its American counterpart. "The stories, the histories, and the myths are utterly interconnected, interdependent."[14] To put it simply, I could not have seen the degree to which the history of early Saskatchewan education was beholden to American antecedents had I not first come of age with Elazar, Kliebard, and Sharp as my cultural staples. Without these intellectual influences, this study lacks its comparative value.

Thacker cites Wallace Stegner's *Wolf Willow* as an example of the "bifurcated perspective" wherein a US author attempts to make sense of his Canadian experience through American eyes.[15] If such a thing is possible, I personify a further trisection – a Canadian writing a history of his home province through the lens of American histories and mythologies, only to argue ultimately that it was not a Canadian experience after all, but a continental one. If this is true, one cannot help but feel somewhat schizophrenic. I am thankful that such a division is entirely an academic one.

That is not to suggest, however, that the westerner does not view himself or herself as distinct from eastern cousins. On those very rare occasions when I do drive to the east, whether on this side of the border or the US side, I inevitably feel that same discomfort I experienced on my first migration to Lexington, Kentucky – that inkling that I have entered a foreign land. Such a sensation abates only when I return to the west, once again to witness that far-distant horizon, bright blue sky, and flatness as far as I can see. For whether I am on the prairies or on the Plains, on the frontier or in the hinterland, I feel no division – no bifurcation. Here, I am whole.

Notes

CHAPTER ONE

1 Prentice, "The American Example."
2 When writing of the American Midwest and the US Plains or Great Plains, it is customary to capitalize these terms for regions. It is not necessary for the Canadian prairies. The continental Great Plains is the transnational region that encompasses both, and I capitalize the term.
3 Rodgers, *Atlantic Crossings.*
4 Sharp, *The Agrarian Revolt,* 4–5.
5 Ibid., vii.
6 Rorty suggests, "Pragmatists think that the history of attempts to isolate the True or the Good, or to define the word 'true' or 'good,' supports their suspicion that there is no interesting work to be done in this area." Such a thought helps me resist any temptation to suggest that this history of Saskatchewan education is better, or truer, than those already extant. In the spirit of pragmatism, I simply confide that my history is different. Rorty's pronouncements on the concept of truth are numerous – here from "Introduction: Pragmatism and Philosophy," xiii. See also "Truth without Correspondence to Reality" and *Philosophy and the Mirror of Nature.*

7 Sewell, Jr, "The Concept of Culture(s)." It is difficult to summarize so prolific a writer but I offer what I perceive to be his main emphases. I am also aware that recent analysis of Sewell's entire body of work by Dylan Riley identifies three phases in his thinking about culture: early cultural turn, high cultural turn, and postcultural turn. Language assumes its greatest prominence, argues Riley, in the middle phase, which corresponds with his work published in his *Logics of History* (2005). See Riley, "The Historical Logic of *Logics of History*," 555–65.

8 American culture and policy were themselves products of transfers from within Rodgers's "North Atlantic community." In my mind, place of origin matters less than where Saskatchewan's policy makers looked for their inspiration. They might, for example, have adopted a British policy but found it in the United States. I designate such an adoption as American.

9 Wolfe, "The Missing Pragmatic Revival," 202.

10 Isern and Shepard, "Duty-free," xxvii–xxxv.

11 Sharp, *Whoop-Up Country*, 4.

12 Ibid., 8.

13 Ibid., 313.

14 Sharp uses "hinterland" for the countryside surrounding Fort Benton, Missouri: "The human stream pouring through Fort Benton was a continuous reminder that the northern plains were the commercial hinterland of the proud little river town." Initially, I thought he might attempt a Laurentian interpretation of development, but, as in his history of the Agrarian Revolt, he sticks with a frontier thesis. My Conclusion returns to the Laurentian and frontier theses as myths of development on the continental Plains. See Sharp, *Whoop-up Country*, 7.

15 For an excellent recent history of the US transcontinental railways, see White, *Railroaded*.

16 White is, if I judge from *Railroaded*, one of those American scholars who, though professing a borderlands perspective, largely ignores the Canadian story.

17 Cohen, *Challenging Orthodoxies*.

18 Brison, *Rockefeller, Carnegie, and Canada*.

CHAPTER TWO

1 Harold Foght writes about students attending rural, village, and town schools as rural, part of an educational system whose fundamental industry is agriculture. See Foght, *Survey*, 77.

2 Canada, Bureau of Statistics, *Census of Prairie Provinces, 1916*, Table X, 154.

3 Canada, Bureau of Statistics, *Sixth Census of Canada, 1921*, Vol. 1, Table 30, 564.

4 Canada, Bureau of Statistics, *Seventh Census of Canada, 1931*, Vol. 1, Table 56, 1010.

5 Ibid., Table 62, 1050–2.

6 Most Canadian high school history texts highlight such causes, so students read that Canadians have never been patriotic or nationalistic, but instead quite practical. For a *typical* view of Confederation, see McInnis, *Canada*, especially chapters 12 and 13. The Province of Canada, New Brunswick, and Nova Scotia combined to create the original four provinces, with Canada splitting into Ontario and Quebec.

7 Lipset, *Continental Divide*, 42.

8 The railway opened in 1885, just in time to help Ottawa quash the Riel Resistance in Saskatchewan.

9 Wilson, "Education in Upper Canada," 192.

10 Gidney, "Upper Canadian Public Opinion."

11 Wilson, "The Ryerson Years in Canada West," 219. For how anti-British and unpatriotic American textbooks were during this period, see Curtis, "Schoolbooks."

12 Ibid., 325–6.

13 Hodgins, *Documentary History*, in Tomkins, "Canadian Education," 11.

14 Smith, "American Culture," in Chaiton and McDonald, eds., *Canadian Schools and Canadian Identity*.

15 Bell also mentions that while Canada was taking in many immigrants, it also had a sizeable outflow of emigrants. This loss of "tradition-carriers," Bell believes, further fragmented Canadian political culture. See Bell and Tepperman, *The Roots of Disunity*, 91–4.

CHAPTER THREE

1 I by no means suggest that the aboriginal or Métis cultures
 in Saskatchewan were irrelevant and unworthy of replication
 by settlers to the region. Unfortunately, indigenous and Métis
 populations were marginalized from mainstream society through a
 variety of mechanisms largely initiated by the federal government
 and supported by the various provincial governments and non-
 aboriginal society generally. Despite the fact the existence of
 indigenous peoples largely disappeared from the historical record
 of Saskatchewan's early schools, as is clear in, for example, the
 Annual Reports by school inspectors to the provincial minister of
 education, the education of Saskatchewan's First Nations and Métis
 students persisted in alternative settings. Today, their influence on
 education is notable and expanding.
2 My conclusions about cultural transfer find corroboration in
 Furlough and Strikwerda, eds., *Consumers against Capitalism?*;
 Laycock: *Populism and Democratic Thought*; Rodgers, *Atlantic
 Crossings*; Sharp, *The Agrarian Revolt*; and Wood, *A History of
 Farmer's Movements in Canada*.
3 Waiser, *Saskatchewan*, 67. The British (35,518) were only slightly
 more numerous than the Americans. Fifty per cent of the
 province's population was born in Canada, and 40 per cent came
 from Ontario. According to Nelson Wiseman, the majority of US
 immigrants to Alberta were of Anglo-Saxon stock, but not those
 who chose Saskatchewan. American and Scandinavian influence
 in Saskatchewan made it far more receptive to socialism than was
 the case in Alberta. See Wiseman, "The Pattern of Prairie Politics,"
 640–60.
4 Waiser, *Saskatchewan*, 69.
5 Sharp, *The Agrarian Revolt*, 4–5.
6 Ibid., 5.
7 Archer, *Saskatchewan*, 119. If one assumes that a family contains
 at minimum two members, Archer documents the movement
 of well over 100,000 Americans to one region of the province.
 The Saskatchewan Valley Land Company employed Colonel A.E.
 Davidson, a former Canadian living in Minnesota, to lead the

recruitment efforts. The town of Davidson, roughly half way between Saskatoon and Regina, bears his name.

8 Shepard, *American Influence*, 6–7.

9 Ibid., 108–10.

10 Widdis, "Borderland Interaction," 115.

11 Elazar, *American Federalism*.

12 Ibid., 86.

13 Ibid., 118. A map labels the dominant political cultures: Colorado, Michigan, Minnesota, North Dakota, Utah, and Wisconsin are predominantly moralistic in orientation, and Idaho, Iowa, Kansas, Montana, and South Dakota, largely moralistic, with individualistic undertones. Nebraska and Wyoming maintain an individualistic, political subculture with moralistic influences.

14 Ibid., 118–19.

15 Turner, *The Frontier In American History*. Turner also accounts for the movement of Americans from the Midwest to the Canadian prairies. "Hundred of thousands of pioneers from the Middle West have crossed the national boundary into Canadian wheat fields eager to find farms for their children, although under an alien flag." Ibid., 109.

16 Widdis, "Borderland Interaction," 119.

17 W.L. Morton, *The Progressive Party*, 30–1.

18 Ibid., 10.

19 Sharp, *The Agrarian Revolt*, 24. Sharp goes so far as to say that virtually every American "society" moved into Canada in one form or another; 25.

20 Ibid., 27.

21 Ibid., 61.

22 According to Sharp, westerners in both countries often attributed North Dakotan Treadwell Twichell's phrase "Go home and slop the hogs" to easterners as an indication of eastern ignorance and lack of regard for the work of the western farmer. Reformers purposefully accused easterners of using the phrase to rouse the ire of their organization's or "society's" members. See ibid., 62.

23 Rodgers writes of the "grand sociological tour" in *Atlantic Crossings*. The purpose of these tours was to study social and civic movements across the North Atlantic community and adapt their

policy solutions. This became a popular outlet for inquiring social reformers at the turn of the twentieth century. As well, social reformers invited key figures from abroad to share their thoughts and experiences. Saskatchewan newspapers frequently mentioned Aaron Sapiro's trips to western Canada to spread the word about cooperatives.

24 Wood, *A History*, 165–6.

25 Sharp, *The Agrarian Revolt*, 57.

26 Advertisements by American manufacturers of farm machinery are mainstays in the *Grain Growers Guide* and *Western Producer*. See also Evans, "The Twine Line," 192.

27 Ibid., 192.

28 See "Soil Products Exposition," 31.

29 MacEwan, *Harvest of Bread*, 82–6.

30 "The Value of Draft Tests for Horses," 23–4. Several leaflets and articles about draft animals appear in the professional correspondence of E.A. Hardy, professor of agricultural engineering, University of Saskatchewan; University of Saskatchewan archives, E.A. Hardy fonds, 4. Horse Pulling Contests.

31 See Saskatchewan, *Annual Report, 1918*, 186. I address this theme more fully in chapter 4.

32 I pursue this level of cultural transfer in chapter 6.

33 Waiser, *Saskatchewan*, 275–6.

34 Ibid., 274.

35 Quote from sdrc.lib.uiowa.edu/traveling-culture/essay.html <5 Nov. 2005>.

36 The Klan first entered Saskatchewan in 1926, although the first organizers in the province fled with the membership fees. Waiser captures the sheer size of the Klan when he compares the number of Klansmen (25,000) and the highest number of members in the Saskatchewan Grain Growers Association (SGGA) in the 1920s (35,000). See Waiser, *Saskatchewan*, 251.

37 Most notable was the Klan's influence on the leader of the province's Conservative party, Dr Anderson. Anderson had served as Saskatchewan's director of education among new Canadians in 1923, and in 1929, as leader of the Conservatives, he launched

an attack on policies of the federal and provincial governments, both Liberal. See ibid., 249–52, and Sharp, *The Agrarian Revolt*, 15 and 95.

38 Arthur S. Morton, *Saskatchewan: The Making of a University*, especially chapter 8. Among the faculty members, the dean of agriculture had first taught at Iowa State College, and the dean of arts and science completed his graduate work at Columbia University. Morton died before completing the manuscript. University of Saskatchewan historian and English professor Carlyle King finished the project and acted as the book's editor.

39 While it is hard to pinpoint those Saskatchewanians who would pursue US university study, between 1923 and 1938 over one thousand Canadians enrolled in graduate study in education at Columbia alone. See Tomkins, *A Common Countenance*, 158. The majority probably emanated from eastern Canada. Westerners were more likely to choose the Midwest, including the University of Chicago.

40 Minutes of a Regular Meeting of the Board of Trustees, Saskatoon School District (henceforth, SSD Minutes), 5 Dec. 1927.

41 Saskatchewan, Annual Report, 1925, 72, 76. See Tomkins, "Foreign Influences," 157–66.

42 The increasing reliance on "the expert" for policy inspiration shows American Progressivism moving into Saskatchewan.

43 Laycock, *Populism and Democratic Thought*, 10.

44 Ibid., 179–89.

45 Cited in Waiser, *Saskatchewan*, 262. Sapiro's greatest achievement in California was helping to create the Sunkist producer's cooperative.

46 Keillor, *Cooperative Commonwealth*, 296–7.

47 The Land O' Lakes dairy cooperative in Minnesota is perhaps the most lasting legacy. See ibid., 300–3.

48 Shepard, *American Influence*, 140.

49 Ibid., 151.

50 Lagemann, *An Elusive Science*, 71. Hanus led a survey of New York City's schools in 1911 and 1912. Lagemann suggests that by 1917 there had been 125 school surveys in the United States, and by 1928, 625. The school survey movement was an outgrowth

of British social research and social policy about the turn of the century. Ibid., 80.

51 See, for example, Anderson, "Rural Educational Problem," 19.

52 Tyack, *The One Best System*, 6–7. Tyack also chronicles the "Rural School Problem" as one requiring solution through modernization and consolidation. See also Cremin, *The Transformation*, 274–6, for a big-picture look at centralization or consolidation.

53 Tyack, *The One Best System*, 193.

54 For Progressivism's reliance on the expert, see Hofstadter, *The Age of Reform*, particularly 131–73.

55 Laycock, *Populism and Democratic Thought*, 577.

56 Ibid., 136.

57 Ibid., 137. Laycock identifies social-democratic influences within the Non-Partisan League (NPL), the United Farmers of Canada (Saskatchewan Section), or UFC, and most significant within the Co-operative Commonwealth Federation (CCF), which formed the provincial government in 1944.

58 Ibid., 20, and in much more detail, 69–135. Radical democrats were visible in the NPL and the UFC and in a host of producer cooperatives across the prairies.

59 Ibid., 23–68. The Progressive Party, the Saskatchewan Grain Growers, and the *Grain Grower's Guide* were the most prominent in displaying this brand of prairie populism. The last form that Laycock identifies is *plebiscitarian* and existed almost entirely in Alberta's Social Credit Party.

60 Sharp, *The Agrarian Revolt*, 40.

61 The Progressives maintained a power base in rural Ontario and the three prairie provinces. The party won 65 seats in the 1921 federal election but only 25 in 1925.

62 McGinnis, *Canada*, 514–18.

63 See Sharp, *The Agrarian Revolt*, 57–66.

64 Roosevelt won 28 per cent of the popular vote and finished second to Woodrow Wilson's 42 per cent. Wilson himself exhibited his own brand of Progressivism. See Wiebe, *The Search for Order*, 216–23.

65 Hofstadter, *The Age of Reform*, 98.

66 Ibid., 137.

67 For an exposé of the travails of John D. Rockefeller, Sr, as head of Standard Oil, see McGerr, *The Rise and Fall*, 157–60.

68 See Laycock, *Populism and Democratic Thought*, 140–4. "'Plutocracy' is an old term of popular movement damnation, and had been common in American Populist and popular discourse since Jefferson. The term refers to more than 'them': it signifies a general understanding of the prevailing political economy, which features financiers, industrialists, large commercial interests, landowners, and railway companies as the winners, and small farmers, urban-working, and lower classes as the losers." Ibid., 78. The Nobel Prize–winning American economist Paul Krugman uses the term frequently in his tweets.

69 See Turner, particularly his essays "The Significance of the Frontier" and "Pioneer Ideals," in Turner, *The Frontier in American History*, 1–38 and 269 – 89, respectively; Lipset, *Agrarian Socialism*; Sharp, *Agrarian Revolt*; Webb, *The Great Plains*; and Worster, *Under Western Skies*.

70 Slotkin, *Gunfighter Nation*, 58–9.

71 Webb, *The Great Plains*, 8.

72 Lipset, *Agrarian Socialism*, 34. For a discussion of how life in the American grain belt influenced life in places such as Minnesota, see Keillor, *Cooperative Commonwealth*.

73 White, *"It's Your Misfortune and None of My Own,"* 184–5.

74 Adams, *Sex in the Snow*.

75 Sewell, Jr, *Work and Revolution*, 10–11.

76 Smith, *Virgin Land*, 37.

77 Ibid., 37.

78 Smith credits St John de Crevecoeur with this sentiment in ibid., 127.

79 Marx, *The Machine*, 99. In 1972, noted Canadian author Margaret Atwood observed that the prevailing theme in Canadian literature is one of survival. This perspective initially seems to agree with Webb and others as to the travails of life beyond the ninety-eighth meridian. However, Atwood does not see the west as any more forbidding than other regions of Canada, including the east. See Atwood, *Survival*.

80 Dippie, "The Moving Finger Writes," 96. The painting is reproduced with the permission of the Autry National Center, Los Angeles, 92; 126.1

81 The most obvious reason is that as long as free US land was still available, settlers would opt for the more fertile soil and temperate climate of the American interior. Once it had "disappeared" and new farming practices encouraged settlement in previously unworkable, arid conditions in both countries, settlement on the Canadian prairies began in earnest.

82 For an American example of the image of the railway, see the engraving *Beyond the Mississippi*, which opens Albert D. Richardson, *Beyond the Mississippi* (1869). See cprr.org/Museum/Through_to_ the_Pacific/Beyond_the_Mississippi.html <18 Feb. 2006>.

83 Friesen, *The Canadian Prairies*, 248–52.

84 Colony settlement was apparent in both countries. Richard White states that a number of these "colonies" segregated themselves into cohesive communities throughout Minnesota and the Dakotas, most notably Swedes and Norwegians. See White, *"It's Your Misfortune ..."*, 194, 299. In Canada, this pattern largely repeated itself, even for American migrants such as the 50,000 families that chose a strip between Regina and Saskatoon. Gerald Friesen notes especially the Mennonite Germans just north of Saskatoon, and a host of Scandinavian settlements. See Friesen, *The Canadian Prairies*, 248–9. While it is difficult to prove that Canadian practices copied US patterns, the end result was largely identical.

85 Although I focused above on the movement of US culture, including a moralistic political culture, particularly from the Midwest and Great Plains, into Saskatchewan, such a transfer was part of a much larger movement of cultures and social policies around what Daniel Rodgers denotes as the North Atlantic community from Bogotá to Berlin. See Rodgers, *Atlantic Crossings*.

CHAPTER FOUR

1 Most school divisions in the province contained one school. Murray, "History of Education," 462. The number of pupils increased from 31,275 in 1906 to 77,000 in 1911.

2 Murray estimates an average of 186 permanent certificates per year between 1906 and 1911; provisional and interim certificates numbered 508 in 1909 and 915 in 1911. Ibid., 463.

3 Ibid., 464. Most of the Saskatchewan trainees worked in rural schools. See Foght, *Survey*, 110.

4 Saskatchewan, Annual Report, 1911, 48.

5 According to J. Donald Wilson, even though between 1812 and 1848 American teachers provided the only instruction that some students received, critics feared that American schoolmasters were corrupting British North American youth. See Wilson, "Education in Upper Canada," 192.

6 Saskatchewan, Annual Report, 1916, 10–11.

7 Ibid., 11.

8 Saskatchewan, Annual Report, 1920, 14.

9 Saskatchewan, Annual Report, 1930, 1.

10 Saskatchewan began certifying qualified American instructors in 1913. Murray, "History of Education" 463.

11 Ibid., 463.

12 Saskatchewan, Annual Report, 1915, 23.

13 Saskatchewan, Annual Report, 1929, 62.

14 Curtis, "Schoolbooks."

15 See, for example, Ontario, *Ontario Normal Schools Manual*, "Science of Education," 1915, http://www.gutenberg.org/files/18451/18451-h/18451-h.htm <19 Feb. 2007>.

16 Horne, *The Philosophy of Education*.

17 See www.answers.com/topic/herman-harrell-horne <21 May 2007>. See also www.talbot.edu/ce20/educators/view.cfm?n=herman_horne <21 May 2007> for a brief biography of Horne.

18 Kliebard, *The Struggle*, 4–8.

19 De Garmo, *Principles*.

20 Kliebard, *The Struggle*, 16–17.

21 Bryan, *The Basis*.

22 Another US textbook, Daniel Putnam's Herbartian *Manual of Pedagogics*, appeared in the normal school's library. The author completed it while principal of the Michigan State Normal School.

23 Keith, *Elementary Education*. Keith was professor of pedagogy and assistant in psychology at North Illinois State Normal School, DeKalb.

24 Kliebard, *The Struggle*, 77-8.

25 Keith, *Elementary Education*, 43.

26 Halleck, *Psychology*. Halleck completed his master's degree at Yale University.

27 Thorndike, *Principles*. Thorndike, of course, was professor at Teacher's College, Columbia University, and one of the foremost proponents of social efficiency.

28 Strayer, *A Brief Course*. Strayer was on faculty at Teacher's College, Columbia University. Kendall and Mirick, *How to Teach*. The authors were commissioners of education for New Jersey. LaRue, *The Science*. LaRue taught at the Normal School of Pennsylvania. Lloyd and Hargreaves, *The Self-Directed School*. Lloyd was professor of education at Wisconsin, and Hargreaves a high school principal in Minneapolis.

29 Saskatchewan, Annual Report, 1916, 28.

30 Foght, *Survey*, 110.

31 Saskatchewan, Annual Report, 1926, 50.

32 Tomkins, *A Common Countenance*, 190. In Canada, the project method became the "enterprise method."

33 George Tomkins estimates that between 1923 and 1938 over one thousand Canadians registered for course work at Columbia University. See Tomkins, "Foreign Influences," 161.

34 The first Saskatchewan normal school opened in Regina in 1913. Normal schools appear in Moose Jaw and Saskatoon in the early 1920s.

35 Gallen, "The Development," 179n4.

36 Saskatchewan, Annual Report, 1912, 45.

37 See Saskatchewan, Annual Report, 1918, 186.

38 Foght, *Survey*, 131.

39 See Saskatchewan, Annual Report, 1918, 192–6.

40 Saskatchewan, Annual Report, 1914, 44.

41 Ibid., 47.

42 Saskatchewan, Annual Report, 1919, 66 and 77, respectively. The visit to the Midwest closely mirrors Walter Murray's in 1906. See chapter 6.

43 SSD Minutes, 23 June 1923. A review of such minutes throughout the 1920s indicates that the district was hiring vocational

instructors consistently, often paying them more than regular classroom teachers.

44 Saskatchewan, Annual Report, 1926, 101.

45 Saskatchewan, Annual Report, 1930, 92–3. Washburne himself would travel to Saskatchewan to spread the word of the Winnetka Plan in the same period.

46 SSD Minutes, 7 July 1930. Miss Amy and Miss Dayton studied at Winnetka in the summer of 1930. On their return to Saskatoon, their supervisor was another attendee, Miss L.G. Marshall, who extended the plan among non-attendees. See SSD Minutes, 21 April 1930.

47 Zilverschmidt, *Changing Schools*, 39–43. Zilverschmidt describes the half-day for the tool subjects as a reflection of G. Stanley Hall's concept of efficiency, while the community centred approach was in keeping with Dewey's philosophy of education.

48 In chapter 3, I suggest that the lag in cultural transfer was closer to 20 years.

49 Saskatchewan, Annual Report, 1919, 59.

50 Patterson, "Progressive Education," 174.

51 The *Alexandra Readers* gradually gave way to *Canadian Readers* beginning in 1923. Saskatchewan, Annual Report, 1923, 13.

52 For an excellent discussion of the role that the *Irish Readers* played in forging curricular knowledge into state knowledge, see Curtis, "Schoolbooks." Nancy Sheehan highlights the *Readers'* moral and religious overtones in "Character Training."

53 Saskatchewan, *Journal of the Legislative Assembly of the Province of Saskatchewan*, Vol. IV, 11 Jan. 1909, 28. Haultain does not explain why he thinks the American Book Company corrupt. Subsequent debates do not reveal any further suggestions by him.

54 Haultain (ibid.) does mention the Canada Publishing Company's readers, but only in regard to price, not content.

55 Ibid., 29. To the western observer, Morang apparently represented "the interests" or the plutocracy.

56 Ibid., 30.

57 In examining the readers, I looked for any shibboleth that might substantiate Haultain's accusations. I found it in the spelling "color" in two poems. I am quite certain there are many others. See

"The Anxious Leaf" in the *Second Book of The Alexandra Readers*, 64–5, and "The Song Sparrows" in the *Fourth Book*, 29.

58 Elazar, *American Federalism*, 117.

59 Ibid., 92. I return to this conception of politics below when discussing local control over education.

60 Sheehan, "Character Training," 79.

61 Ibid., 78.

62 Saskatchewan, Annual Report, 1908, 17.

63 Saskatchewan, Annual Report, 1917, 11.

64 The Historical Textbook Collection in the Education Library, University of Saskatchewan, displays readers from across the province and, indeed, across the continent. I examined a number and concluded that some were in use in schools, though when is difficult to pinpoint. Those that bore the stamp of a normal school and/or a specific school division in Saskatchewan were, I concluded, in use in the province's schools. Others, such as the *Horace Mann Readers*, bore no stamp and appeared to have been used in New York.

65 Saskatchewan, Annual Report, 1911, 44. The following year the same inspector authorized destruction of about one thousand readers.

66 Flagg-Young and Field, *The Young and Field Literary Readers*. These readers bore the stamp of the normal school in Saskatoon. On Ella Flagg-Young's attachment to John Dewey, see Cremin, *The Transformation*, 135–6.

67 Fasset, *The Beacon Fifth Reader*. This displayed the stamp of the Regina Normal School.

68 Crane and Wheeler, *Wheeler's Graded Literary Readers with Interpretations*. These were from the library of the Moose Jaw Normal School.

69 Dressel, Robins, and Graff, *The New Barnes Readers*. The Grand Central School Division used this. Girman and Maltby, *The Winston Readers*. This held the stamp of Moose Jaw's normal school.

70 Cohen, *Challenging Orthodoxies*, 89. I discuss this concept in detail below.

71 Cohen's discussion of languages of discourse relies on the postmodern "linguistic turn."

72 Langley, *The Programs*, 173. The first version I found in the

Historical Textbook Collection was Duncan, *The Story of the Canadian People*.

73 See Langley, *The Programs*, 269–91.
74 See Tomkins, *A Common Countenance*, 175, and von Heyking, *Creating Citizens*, 32–3.
75 Kliebard, *The Struggle*, 180–1.
76 Coulter, "Getting Things Done," 669–99.
77 Patterson, "Progressive Education."
78 The evidence includes photographs of teachers and students in class, textbooks teachers used, students' recollections of their school experience, teachers' reports on how they taught, reports from outsiders who visited classrooms, students' writings in yearbooks and newspapers, research studies of teaching practices, and descriptions of classroom architecture. See Cuban, *How Teachers Taught*, 13.
79 Ibid., 142–4.
80 Hallman, "Telling Tales," 156–7.
81 SSD Minutes, 22 March 1930.
82 Cather, "The Best Years," 81–2.
83 This is only a portion of what Dewey would describe as a recitation. In *How We Think*, he outlined a powerful model that included five phases: preparation and presentation, but also comparison, generalization, and application. The three final phases were to engage the student in extensive thinking, not just repeating. Today educators would characterize them as higher-order thinking. As with much of Dewey's philosophy, it was misunderstood and often misapplied. See *How We Think*, 201–2.
84 Kliebard, *The Struggle* 7.
85 Ibid., 7–8.
86 Stegner, *Wolf Willow*, 81.

CHAPTER FIVE

1 Saskatchewan, Annual Report, 1917, 100.
2 Stamp, "Education," 320. In so easily dismissing Foght's recommendation, Stamp betrays the mentality that Foght sought to expunge – the notion that urban education took precedence over rural.

3 Noonan, "Saskatchewan Separate Schools," 27.

4 Milner, "Valley Christian Academy," 111–12.

5 Funk, "The Origin."

6 Lears, *Rebirth*, 133–4.

7 Foght, *The School System of Ontario*, 10

8 Lears, *Rebirth*, 158.

9 Postel, *The Populist Vision*, 46–9.

10 Ohles, Ohles, and Ramsay, *Biographical Dictionary*, 113–14.

11 White, *"It's Your Misfortune ... "*, particularly chapter 14.

12 See links.jstor.org/sici?sici=0002-7162(191203)40%3C149%3ATCS%3 E2.0.CO%3B2-I <3 June 2007>.

13 See www-distance.syr.edu/stubblefield.html <3 June 2007>.

14 See webs.wichita.edu/?u=pcampbell&p=past presidents <3 June 2007>.

15 Foght, *Rural School*. See www.archive.org/stream/ ruralschoolcons000fogh#page/n3/mode/2up <11 April 2011>.

16 Ibid., 3.

17 Foght, *Rural Denmark*, www.onread.com/reader/87749/ <11 April 2011>.

18 Ibid., 24.

19 Foght, *Survey*, 5.

20 Foght, *The School System of Ontario, 41*.

21 My inspiration for this approach comes from Sol Cohen's examination of language and educational discourse and how changes in language signal a shift in the forms of education. In "Language and History," he explains how a change in language signalled a movement from a traditional approach to education (evident in the language of William Torrey Harris) towards a more Progressive form, as the language of John Dewey reveals. My task is simpler: to reveal how the adoption of American meanings of the school, particularly the rural school, and the language of reform signal an American bent in Saskatchewan education that historians have yet to acknowledge. See Cohen, "Language and History," in *Challenging Orthodoxies*.

22 Foght, *Survey*, 7.

23 See Kingdon, *Agendas*, for an outstanding discussion of where policies come from and why.

24 Laycock, *Populism*, 14. These ideologies include liberalism, conservatism, and socialism.

25 Hofstadter, *The Age of Reform*, and Elazar, *American Federalism*.

26 See Hofstadter, *The Age of Reform*, 60–93.

27 Ibid., 7.

28 See Laycock, *Populism*, 3–21. Much of what Laycock identifies as central to prairie populism is almost identical to Elazar's *moralistic* political cultural subgroup.

29 Cohen, *Challenging Orthodoxies*, 89. I encourage the reader to monitor the language of efficiency that appears in many of the quotations in this chapter.

30 Tyack, *The One Best System*, 23.

31 Cubberly, *Rural Life*, 167.

32 Foght, *The American Rural School*, 2.

33 Ibid., 304.

34 Ibid., 17.

35 Ibid., 324.

36 Ibid., 325.

37 Carney, *Country Life*, 148. Cremin suggests that Carney's book became standard reading for rural teachers; *Transformation*, 84n.

38 Saskatchewan, Annual Report, 1913, 62.

39 Saskatchewan, Annual Report, 1916, 113.

40 Foght, *Survey*, 25.

41 Ibid., 27–8.

42 Saskatchewan, Annual Report, 1920, 19.

43 Saskatchewan, Annual Report, 1913, 63-4.

44 Saskatchewan, *Consolidated Schools in Saskatchewan*, 5.

45 Ibid., 7.

46 Foght, *Survey*, 172.

47 Ibid., 5.

48 This process began with the National Education Association's Committee of Twelve on the Rural School Problem. See Tyack, *The One Best System*, 23.

49 Callahan, *Education*, 112.

50 Tyack and Cuban, *Tinkering*, 18. Ellen Condliffe Lagemann chronicles the launch of the school survey movement in the 1890s, when "school administrators had become increasingly concerned with finding ways to gather precise information about the 'efficiency' of the schools." See Lagemann, *An Elusive Science*, 79.

51 Tyack and Cuban, *Tinkering*, 17.

52 Kliebard identifies Cubberly as a social efficiency educator. See Kliebard, *The Struggle*, 191.

53 Not surprising, Inspector Kennedy of Weyburn, who religiously attended the annual conventions of the National Education Association, was already aware of efficiency in education before the arrival of Foght. In 1913, he wrote in his annual report, "The efficiency of your school is not to be measured by the number of students who pass their examinations but by the provision that is made for the education of every child in the district and the solid foundation laid for future citizenship. We must keep in mind the fact that the great majority of our pupils are not going into the High Schools but into actual business of some kind or other; we should then prepare them for the life they must live, so that they may be intelligent and useful citizens." Saskatchewan, *Annual Report, 1913*, 43.

54 Foght, *Survey*, 57.

55 Ibid., 81.

56 Saskatchewan, Annual Report, 1911, 54.

57 Saskatchewan, Annual Report, 1914, 71.

58 Lagemann, *An Elusive Science*, 79.

59 Kliebard, *The Struggle*, 77-8.

60 Foght, *Survey*, 88.

61 Ibid., 73.

62 Ibid., 131.

63 Ibid., 19.

64 Annual Reports chronicled the evolution of these divisions within the Department of Education. The legislature passed the Vocational Education Act in 1920. From among these new divisions, for example, Fannie Twiss, provincial director of household science, took a year's leave to take a course in home economics at Columbia in 1920. See Saskatchewan, Annual Report, 1920, 81. Providing sabbatical leaves to provincial educationists was another of Foght's recommendations.

65 Saskatchewan, Vocational Education Act, 1919–1920, c. 42, s. 3.

66 Saskatchewan, Annual Report, 1923, 14.

67 Ibid., 98.

68 Saskatchewan, Annual Report, 1922, 79.

69 Rodgers denotes a similar American misinterpretation of European social policy, which often lost some of its meaning in transit. He blames latecomers to the social policy process in the North Atlantic community – often Amercians – who witnessed only the end product, but not the process. As I argue throughout chapters 3 and 4, policies appeared in Saskatchewan some 10 to 20 years following their US adoption. Their makers came late to education policy, as is clear from their adoption of the language of social efficiency some 20 years following its US introduction. See Rodgers, *Atlantic Crossings*.

70 In one inspector's report, the order in which he chronicles various aspects of his inspections is itself quite telling. He discusses students and teachers near mid-report, well after the length of school term, buildings, school grounds, heating, and water supply. Teachers appeared between "Toilets" and "Progress of Pupils." See Saskatchewan, Annual Report, 1919, 119.

71 SSD Minutes, 3 Oct. 1927.

72 For a very negative assessment of the intention behind intelligence testing within American education, see Nasaw, *Schooled to Order*, particularly chapter 9.

73 Saskatchewan, Annual Report, 1923, 97.

74 SSD Minutes, 19 March 1928.

75 Patterson, "Society, " 374. The pursuit of greater efficiency in education seems to me a sign of American-style Progressivism at work in Canadian schools. Patterson's definition of Progressive is much narrower than that of such historians as Kliebard and Cremin.

76 See Kliebard, *The Struggle*, 155–78.

77 In 1929, five other Saskatchewan teachers completed the summer course in Winnetka.

78 Saskatchewan, Annual Report, 1930, 96.

CHAPTER SIX

1 University Act, 1907.

2 A "land grant" university is one that received a large tract of land from a US state, often in conjunction with federal assistance, to increase access to higher education for its residents. The expansion

of land grant universities signalled a democratization in higher education while making it more utilitarian. Thelin, *A History*, 75–6.

3 One might suggest that Murray's devotion bordered on obsession, almost a personal crusade. He assured the university's place among the "greats" of North America, but also inextricably linked his own stature and status with that of the institution.

4 Veysey, *The Emergence*.

5 Ibid., 12.

6 Kerr, *The Uses*, 46–7. For a somewhat contrary view, see Levine, *The American College*. For the development of agrarian populism in the United States and Canada, see Lipset, *Agrarian Socialism*, and Sharp, *The Agrarian Revolt*.

7 Clyde Barrow assumes a Marxist perspective and suggests that this phase in American higher education saw the employment of the university as a tool of the elite business class to create a corporate ideal among mainstream American citizens. As such, it joined the "ideological state apparatus." See Barrow, *Universities and the Capitalist State*.

8 Levine estimates that two thirds of all students sought preparation for a specific profession following graduation. See Levine, *The American College*, 40–3.

9 Veysey, *The Emergence*, 306–10. The corporate nature of American higher education is a prime focus of Barrow's work.

10 This was also to be the case at the University of Saskatchewan in 1919.

11 See Levine, *The American College*, 162–84.

12 Hutchins, *The Higher Learning*, 43, as cited in Levine, *The American College*, 90.

13 See Barrow, *Universities*, 186-220.

14 *Employment* versus *tenure* was a prominent issue in US higher education and would become equally so at the University of Saskatchewan.

15 Rudolph, *The American College*, 432.

16 Thelin, *A History*, 238–9, and Barrow, *Universities*, 84–5.

17 Arthur S. Morton, *Saskatchewan*, 37.

18 Murray himself had been on faculty at Dalhousie University in Halifax, Nova Scotia, prior to his appointment at Saskatchewan.

19 Arthur S. Morton, *Saskatchewan*, 59. Morton did not complete his manuscript before his death; Carlyle King assembled and edited the manuscript.

20 Ibid., 58. Although the institution borrowed the design from St Louis, the architects hailed from Montreal.

21 Thelin, *A History*, xx.

22 Veysey, *The Emergence*, 310.

23 Hayden, *Seeking a Balance*, 35.

24 Ibid., 116.

25 I leave this discussion for a subsequent section.

26 He alone was able to lobby the province to block creation of a second university in Regina. He was the main reason the capital did not gain a university until much later. The Univeristy of Regina became an independent, degree-granting institution in 1974. Murray's efforts at eliminating competition were entirely in keeping with the expectations of the Carnegie Foundation, whose board he sat on several times.

27 Hayden, *Seeking a Balance*, 35–6.

28 Arthur S. Morton, *Saskatchewan*, 66–78.

29 A. Ross Hill to Walter C. Murray, 8 Sept. 1908, University of Saskatchewan Archives, Jean Murray Collection, A.IV.82.

30 University of Saskatchewan Archives, College of Agriculture, (I) Dean's Correspondence, A. Reports to the President, 1912–1928, folder 1. 11 May 1916, 2–3.

31 Rutherford also belonged to several US agricultural organizations, including the Dryland Farming Congress, which met annually in venues across the continent. Shepard notes that he preceded the provincial minister of agriculture as Saskatchewan's representative with the Congress. See Shepard, *American Influence*, 240.

32 I compiled these details from several pieces of Dean Rutherford's correspondence with the president, in University of Saskatchewan Archives, College of Agriculture (I), Dean's Correspondence, A. Reports to the President, 1912–1928.

33 Howard J. Savage, "Supplementary Memorandum on the U of S," 15 Oct. 1928, 13, University of Saskatchewan Archives, President's Office fonds, Walter C. Murray fonds, B, vol. 21.

34 Dean Rutherford to President Murray, 15 Nov. 1915, 5, and 28 Nov. 1918, 1–2, respectively, in University of Saskatchewan Archives,

College of Agriculture, (I) Dean's Correspondence, A. Reports to the President, 1912–1928. For the 1912 reference, see Dean Rutherford to Dean, College of Agriculture, Ohio State University, 8 April 1912, University of Saskatchewan Archives, College of Agriculture, (I) Dean's Correspondence, C. Addresses and Articles, 9, Agricultural Short Courses.

35 Rutherford had earlier taught at Iowa State College and the University of Manitoba. Morton, *Saskatchewan*, 83.

36 It shocked many people who helped create the University of Saskatchewan, including Murray himself, when the province did not select Regina for the site, particularly since the Wisconsin Idea connected the state university to the state capital in Madison. They had assumed that geographical proximity would assist requests for, and granting of, funding. Murray's personal papers also convey his assumption that Regina would be the choice.

37 As cited in Murray and Murray, *The Prairie Builder*, 81.

38 Hayden, *Seeking a Balance*, 121.

39 See Levine, *The American College*, 162–84

40 Brison, *Rockefeller*, especially 43–65.

41 W.M. Gilbert, Esq., to Walter Murray, 3 Nov. 1916, University of Saskatchewan Archives, Jean Murray Collection, A.IV.14.

42 Thelin, *A History*, 239.

43 As cited in Murray and Murray, *The Prairie Builder*, 191. Frank Vanderlip of the Carnegie Foundation said in 1908 that he saw no purpose in "useless competition." Murray clearly agreed. See Barrow, *Universities*, 82. Barrow also chronicles the "survey movement" in several states, the results of which rejected the notion of inefficient duplication or fragmentation of education in New England; 99–100.

44 Brison, *Rockefeller*, 49.

45 Ibid., 59–60.

46 scaa.usask.ca/gallery/uofs_events/articles/1926.php <3 Dec. 2007>.

47 Murray and Murray, *The Prairie Builder*, 179–80. Barrow would probably see membership in the Pension Fund as part of a larger market to allow the free flow of *employees* among campuses anywhere in the United States and Canada. See Barrow, *Universities*, 84.

48 Murray and Murray, *The Prairie Builder*, 180.

49 Ibid., 196.

50 Walter C. Murray to J.P. Keppel, President of the Carnegie Foundation, 27 Nov. 1931, University of Saskatchewan Archives, Jean Murray Collection, A.IV.14.

51 Dr. R.M. Lester to Walter C. Murray, 18 Nov. 1934, ibid.

52 Barrow, *Universities*, 16.

53 When Murray's presidency ended, so did Carnegie financial support.

54 Murray did not perform his duties for the 1919–20 academic year.

55 The public outcry over the firing of the four resulted in appointment of a visitor to whom the university's constitution gave authority to investigate the matter. See Judgement of the Visitor, Statutes of the University of Saskatchewan, 1920, as cited at scaa.usask.ca/gallery/uofs_events/articles/1919.php <1 June 2013>.

56 See Murray and Murray, *The Prairie Builder*, 107–34, and Hayden, *Seeking a Balance*, 78–116.

57 Murray and Murray, *The Prairie Builder*, 116–17.

58 Ibid., 116. Murray's pronouncements on academic freedom and responsibility resemble Barrow's "managerial conception" in *Universities*, 195–9.

59 The Co-operative Commonwealth Federation, or CCF, was a social-democratic political party beginning to emerge in Saskatchewan and would later form the provincial government. It and its successor, the New Democratic Party (NDP), held power, save for Ross Thatcher's Liberals (1964–71) and Grant Devine's Conservatives (1982–91), until the Saskatchewan Party, descendant of the provincial Conservatives, assumed office in 2007. The CCF also became a national party, and the NDP currently forms the official opposition in Ottawa.

60 See *The Sheaf*, 30 Sept. 1938. Carlyle King would later write a history of research at the university; *Extending the Boundaries*, however, does not mention the boundaries of freedom of speech.

61 See Barrow, *Universities*, 246.

62 Veysey, *The Emergence*, 108.

63 Murray, "Report of the President, 1908–1909," 2.

64 The Saskatchewan trio visited the University of Manitoba in Winnipeg, several universities in Ontario, and the Universities of Illinois, Indiana, Iowa, Michigan, Minnesota, Missouri, and Wisconsin. On the return trip, they toured Washington University in St Louis, Missouri, and the University of Chicago.

65 Murray to Sir Robert Falconer, 22 Feb. 1930, as cited in Hayden, *Seeking a Balance*, 35.

66 Murray, "Report of the President, 1908–1909," 3. Murray also noted that President Snyder of the Michigan Agricultural College, a long-time champion of separation from the larger campus, favoured a unified campus for new countries or territories.

67 Hayden, *Seeking a Balance*, 37.

68 G.C. Creelman to Walter Murray, 8 Oct. 1908, University of Saskatchewan Archives, Jean Murray Collection, A.IV.82.

69 A. Ross Hill to Walter C. Murray, 8 Sept. 1908, 3–4, ibid.

70 D.A. Houston to Walter C. Murray, 4 Nov. 1908, 1, ibid.

71 Walter C. Murray, "Report respecting the principles which determine the location of a University," Regina, 29 Jan. 1909, 5, ibid.

72 Ibid. In all, Murray's report cites six American "University men" at the foundation for his proposal to the board of governors. It noted only one Canadian source: Principal Robertson of the Macdonald School of Agriculture, McGill University, in Montreal.

73 From scaa.usask.ca/gallery/uofs_events/articles/1909php <28 Dec. 2007>.

74 It is difficult to judge how the university's location affected its relations with, and influence on, the provincial government in Regina.

75 Morton, *Saskatchewan*, 81.

76 Murray and Murray, *The Prairie Builder*, 67.

77 Hayden, *Seeking a Balance*, 66.

78 Ibid., 67.

79 For American developments in professional education, see Levine, *The American College*, 45–67.

80 Hayden, *Seeking a Balance*, 126–8.

81 King, *Extending the Boundaries*.

82 I use the term *social efficiency* in the same way as Herbert Kliebard, who sees its advocates making up one of four interest groups all vying for pre-eminence within the larger Progressive movement. Kliebard looks at the period 1900–20 as its heyday. See Kliebard, *The Struggle for the American Curriculum*, particularly 77–131.

83 Levine, *The American College*, 18.

84 See Barrow, *Universities*, 12–59. Unlike many large American

universities, however, which placed business people and members of the social elite on boards of governors, no such elite existed on the Canadian prairies. This chapter looks below at the dangers of applying a US business model out of context.

85 One exception: the innovative ways in which Canadian universities recruited and mobilized when war started in summer 1914 (the United States entered only in April 1917). The small, multi-ethnic University of Saskatchewan probably borrowed practices from much larger, mainly Anglo-Saxon eastern universities.

86 Murray, "Report of the President, 1908–1909," 6.

87 American writers in the pastoral tradition identify westward movement as key to a simpler life, free of the trials and tribulations of the more complex and conflict-ridden east. These writers also suggest that American writers idealize western life and equate western expansion with producing a society or way of life superior to its easterly precursor. See Marx, *The Machine in the Garden*, and Smith, *Virgin Land*.

88 See Slotkin, *Regeneration*, 8–9.

CHAPTER SEVEN

1 Widdis writes that the Department of Immigration deployed American mythology of the agrarian ideal to lure US farmers to the Canadian west. See "Border Interaction," 111.

2 Rodgers, *Atlantic Crossings*.

3 Foght, *The American Rural School*, 302.

4 Ibid., 329–30.

5 Cubberly, *Rural Life*, 166–7. "City-educated and city-trained teachers have talked of the city, over-emphasized the affairs of the city, and sighed to get back to the city to teach."

6 Ibid., 170–1.

7 Foght, *The American Rural School*, 16–17.

8 Ibid., 303.

9 Foght, "The Country School," 149–50.

10 Foght, *Survey*, 20.

11 Carney, *Country Life*, 134.

12 Ibid., 136.

13 Tyack, *The One Best System*, 15–16.

14 Ibid., 17.

15 Ibid., 17.

16 Raban, *Bad Land*, 162.

17 I return to this theme at the end of this section.

18 Saskatchewan, Annual Report, 1913, 62.

19 Saskatchewan, Annual Report, 1914, 63.

20 Foght, *Survey*, 29.

21 Ibid., 32.

22 Saskatchewan, Annual Report, 1914, 48.

23 Saskatchewan, Annual Report, 1912, 45.

24 Saskatchewan, Annual Report, 1915, 50.

25 Saskatchewan, Annual Report, 1913, 43.

26 Ibid., 90.

27 Charyk, *The Little White Schoolhouse*, back cover.

28 Tyack, *The One Best System*, 24.

29 Saskatchewan, Annual Report, 1927, 92.

30 Saskatchewan, Annual Report, 1924, 76.

31 SSD Minutes, 7 June 1927. At the time of Snell's statement, there existed two public school boards – one for elementary schools and one for collegiates – but also at least one for the Separate School Division.

32 See, for example, the statement on page 96 above from Foght, *Rural School Consolidation in Missouri*.

33 For an argument in favour of consolidation, see Kennedy, *Rural Life*. Kennedy was a professor at the University of North Dakota and based much of his discussion on his own childhood in the state.

34 Funk, "The Origin," 43–9. The cost of conveyance in rural Saskatchewan was about three times that of most rural American states.

35 Ibid., 48.

36 White, *"It's Your Misfortune ..."*, 299.

37 See Tyack, *The One Best System*, and Lipset, "The Ideology of Local Control."

38 Stevenson, *Unfulfilled Union*.

39 US census data confirm that both North Dakota and South Dakota

had an even larger urban–rural divide early in the century than did Saskatchewan. North Dakota, for example, was 89 per cent rural in 1910, 86.4 per cent in 1920, and 83.4 per cent in 1930. None the less rural schools were consolidating by 1918. See www.census.gov/population/census data/urpop0090.txt <19 Feb. 2008>.

40 Foght, *Survey*, 5.

41 Waiser, *Saskatchewan*, 498–9. In 1971, a slim majority of Saskatchewan inhabitants were urban (53 per cent).

42 Lipset, *Agrarian Socialism*, 33.

43 Tyack, *The One Best System*, 24.

44 Funk, "The Origin," 58.

45 Scharf, "An Historical Overview," 9. See also, in the same volume, Owen, "Towards a New Day," 37.

46 Courtney, "The Ideology," 47–8.

47 Lipset, *Agrarian Socialism*, 32–3.

48 Lipset, "The Ideology," 33.

49 Elazar, *American Federalism*, 91.

50 Ibid., 92.

51 Sewell, Jr, "The Concept(s)," 53.

52 Brooks, "Liberal Education," 103–17.

53 See Postel, *The Populist Vision*, 45–68.

54 See www.wisconsinidea.wisc.edu/history.html <10 May 2011>.

55 For an excellent discussion of how seemingly well-intentioned Progressive, urban reformers in the American south encountered robust resistance from control-minded rural patrons, see Link, *The Paradox*. Link shows how the paternalism of the reformers, many of whom viewed the practices of the country folks as backward, appeared to the rural folks an external threat to local control over local affairs.

56 A. Kennedy to Dean Rutherford, 17 July 1916, University of Saskatchewan Archives, College of Agriculture, (I) Dean's Correspondence D. Dean Rutherford's Correspondence I. General, 1911–1917, folder 23. Kennedy's estimate of 94 per cent bears striking resemblance to Foght's estimate that 95 per cent of rural American stuents do not go beyond the district school. See quotation from p. 102 above.

CHAPTER EIGHT

1 SSD Minutes, 3 March 1930.
2 Owen, "Towards a New Day," 45.
3 Gallen, "The Development," 166.
4 Hansen et al., "Comprehensive Secondary Schools," 1, www.edu.
   uwo.ca/technology/comprehensive.pdf <24 May 2011>.
5 See Kliebard, *The Struggle*, particularly 106–31 and 205–30.
6 See Brison, *Rockefeller*, 197–202.
7 I refer, of course, to Patricia Limerick's *Something in the Soil*, where
   she continues a "new" history of the west, which includes only the
   American west.
8 Higham and Thacker, *One West, Two Myths: A Comparative Reader*
   and *One West: Two Myths II.*
9 Francis, "Turner versus Innis."
10 Katerberg, "A Northern Vision."
11 Worster: "Two Faces West."
12 Comparative historians agree that the Laurentian thesis gained
   little foothold among American historians. The one obvious
   exception is relatively recent: William Cronon, *Nature's Metropolis.*
13 Sharp, *The Agrarian Revolt*, viii.
14 Thacker, "Introduction," 11.
15 Ibid., 10.

References

ARCHIVAL SOURCES

Library and Archives Canada
University of Saskatchewan Archives. Dean of Agriculture fonds
– Jean Murray Collection
– President's Office fonds
– Special Collections
Washington University Libraries, St Louis, Missouri, University
　　Archives, Department of Special Collections
Wichita State University Libraries, Wichita, Kansas, Special
　　Collections and University Archives

BOOKS AND ARTICLES

Adams, Michael. *Sex in the Snow: Canadian Social Values at the End of
　　the Millennium*. Toronto: Penguin Books, 1998.
Archer, John H. *Saskatchewan: A History*. Saskatoon: Western Producer
　　Books, 1980.
Atwood, Margaret. *Survival: A Thematic Guide to Canadian Literature*.
　　Toronto: McClelland and Stewart, 2004.
Barrow, Clyde. *Universities and the Capitalist State: Corporate
　　Liberalism and the Reconstruction of American Higher Education*.
　　Madison: University of Wisconsin Press, 1990.

Bell, David, and Lorne Tepperman. *The Roots of Disunity: A Look at Canadian Political Culture*. Toronto: McClelland and Stewart, 1979.

Bowers, C.A., Ian Housego, and Doris Dyke, eds. *Education and Social Policy: Local Control of Education*. New York: Random House, 1970.

Brison, Jeffrey D. *Rockefeller, Carnegie, and Canada: American Philanthropy and the Arts and Letters in Canada*. Montreal: McGill-Queen's University Press, 2005.

Brooks, Kevin. "Liberal Education on the Great Plains: American Experiments, Canadian Flirtations, 1930–1950." *Great Plains Quarterly* 17 (spring 1997): 103–17.

Bryan, Elmer Burrit. *The Basis of Practical Teaching: A Book in Pedagogy*. New York: Silver Burdett, 1905.

Callahan, Raymond E. *Education and the Cult of Efficiency: A Study of the Social Forces That Have Shaped the Administration of the Public Schools*. Chicago: University of Chicago Press, 1962.

Carney, Mabel. *Country Life and the Country School: A Study of the Agencies of Rural Progress and of the Social Relationship of the School to the Country Community*. Chicago: Row, Peterson and Company, 1912.

Cather, Willa. *The Old Beauty and Others*. New York: Alfred A. Knopf, 1948.

Chaiton, Alf, and Neil McDonald, eds. *Canadian Schools and Canadian Identity*. Toronto: Gage Educational Publishing, 1977.

Charyk, John C. *The Little White Schoolhouse*. Saskatoon: Prairie Books, 1984.

Cochrane, Don, ed. *So Much for the Mind*. Toronto: Kagan and Woo, 1987.

Cohen, Sol. "Language and History: A Perspective on School Reform Movements and Change in Education." In Sol Cohen, *Challenging Orthodoxies: Toward a New Cultural History of Education*, 87–104. New York: Peter Lang, 1999.

Coulter, Rebecca Priegent. "Getting Things Done: Donalda J. Dickie and Leadership through Practice." *Canadian Journal of Education* 28 no. 4 (2005): 669–99.

Courtney, John C. "The Ideology of Local Control: A Reply." In Bowers, Housego, and Dyke, eds., *Education and Social Policy*, 43–50.

Crane, William Iler, and William Henry Wheeler. *Wheeler's Graded*

Literary Readers with Interpretations. Chicago: W.H. Wheeler & Co.,
  1919.

Cremin, Lawrence A. *The Transformation of the School: Progressivism
  in American Education, 1876–1957.* New York: Vintage Books, 1964.

Cronon, William. *Nature's Metropolis: Chicago and the Great West.* New
  York: W.W. Norton, 1991.

Cuban, Larry. *How Teachers Taught: Constancy and Change in American
  Classrooms, 1880–1990.* New York: Teacher's College Press, 1993.

Cubberly, Elwood. *Rural Life and Education: A Study of the Rural School
  Problem as a Phase of the Rural-Life Problem.* Boston: Houghton
  Mifflin, 1914.

Curtis, Bruce. "Schoolbooks and the Myth of Curricular Republicanism:
  The State and the Curriculum in Canada West, 1820–1850." *Histoire
  social – Social History* 16 no. 32 (Nov. 1983): 305–29.

De Garmo, Charles. *Principles of Secondary Education.* New York:
  MacMillan, 1907.

Dewey, John. *How We Think.* Mineola, NY: Dover Press, 1997.

Dippie, Brian W. "The Moving Finger Writes: Western Art and the
  Dynamics of Change." In Prown et al, eds., *Discovered Lands,
  Invented Pasts: Transforming Visions of the American West*, 89–115.
  New Haven, Conn.: Yale University Press, 1992.

Dressel, Herman, May Robbins, and Ellis U. Graff. *The New Barnes
  Readers: The Kearney Plan.* Chicago: Laidlaw Brothers, 1924.

Duncan, David M. *The Story of the Canadian People.* Toronto:
  MacMillan Company, 1919.

Elazar, Daniel J. *American Federalism: A View from the States.* New
  York: Thomas Y. Crowell Co., 1966.

Evans, Sterling. "The Twine Line: Mexican Henequen, U.S.–Canadian
  Relations, and Binder Twine in the Northern Plains and Prairie
  Provinces, 1890–1950." In Sterling Evans, ed., *The Borderlands of
  the American and Canadian Wests: Essay on Regional History of the
  Forty-ninth Parallel*, 189–202. Lincoln: University of Nebraska Press,
  2006.

Fasset, James H. *The Beacon Fifth Reader.* Boston: Ginn and Company,
  1918.

Flagg-Young, Ella, and Walter Taylor Field. *The Young and Field Literary
  Readers.* Boston: Ginn and Long, 1914.

Foght, Harold W. *A Survey of Education in the Province of Saskatchewan, Canada*. Regina: King's Printer, 1918.

– *Rural Denmark and Its Schools*. Boston: MacMillan Co., 1915.

– *Rural School Consolidation in Missouri*. First District Normal School: 1913.

– *The American Rural School: Its Characteristics, Its Future and Its Problems*. New York: Macmillan, 1910.

– "The Country School." *Annals of the American Academy of Political and Social Science* 40 (March 1912): 149–57.

– *The School System of Ontario with Special Reference to the Rural Schools*. Washington: Government Printing Office, 1915.

Fourth Book of the Alexandra Readers. Toronto: McMillan, 1908

Francis, R. Douglas, and Howard Palmer, eds. *The Prairie West: Historical Readings*. Edmonton: Pica Pica Press, 1992.

– "Turner versus Innis: Two Mythic Wests." In Higham and Thacker, eds., *One West, Two Myths Vol. II*, 15–28.

Friesen, Gerald. *The Canadian Prairies: A History*. Toronto: University of Toronto Press, 1991.

Funk, Jack. "The Origin and Development of Consolidated School Districts in Saskatchewan." Master's thesis, University of Saskatchewan, 1971.

Furlough, Ellen, and Carl Strikwerda, eds. *Consumers against Capitalism? Consumer Cooperation in Europe, North American, and Japan, 1840–1990*. Lanham, Md.: Rowman & Littlefield, 1999.

Gallen, Verna. "The Development of the Teaching Profession in Saskatchewan." In Brian Noonan, Dianne Hallman, and Murray Scharf, eds., *A History of Education in Saskatchewan: Selected Readings*, 165–80. Regina: Canadian Plains Research Centre, 2006.

Gidney, R. D. "Upper Canadian Public Opinion and Common School Improvement in the 1830's." *Histoire sociale – Social History* 5 no. 9 (April 1972): 48–60.

Girman, Sidney G., and Ethel H. Maltby. *The Winston Readers*. Philadelphia: John C. Winston Co., 1918.

Halleck, Rueben Post. *Psychology and Psychic Culture*. New York: American Book Company, 1895.

Hayden, Michael. *Seeking a Balance: The University of Saskatchewan, 1907–1982*. Vancouver: University of British Columbia Press, 1983.

Higham, C.L., and Robert Thacker, eds. *One West, Two Myths: A Comparative Reader*. Calgary: University of Calgary Press, 2004.

–, eds., *One West: Two Myths II: Essays on Comparison*. Calgary: University of Calgary Press, 2006.

Hofstadter, Richard. *The Age of Reform from Bryan to F.D.R.* New York: Vintage Books, 1955.

Horne, Herman Harrell. *The Philosophy of Education, Being the Foundations in the Related Natural and Mental Sciences*. New York: Macmillan, 1904.

Hutchins, Robert M. *The Higher Learning in America*. New Haven, Conn.: Yale University Press, 1936.

Isern, Thomas D., and R. Bruce Shepard. "Duty Free: An Introduction to the Practice of Regional History along the Forty-ninth Parallel." In Sterling Evans, ed., *The Borderlands of the American and Canadian Wests: Essay on Regional History of the Forty-ninth Parallel*, xxvii–xxxv. Lincoln: University of Nebraska Press, 2006.

Katerberg, William H., "A Northern Vision: Frontiers and the West in the Canadian and American Imagination." In Higham and Thacker, eds., *One West, Two Myths II*, 63–83.

Keillor, Steven J. *Cooperative Commonwealth: Co-ops in Rural Minnesota, 1859–1939*. St Paul: Minnesota Historical Society Press, 2000.

Keith, John A.H. *Elementary Education: Its Problems and Processes*. Chicago: Foresman and Co., 1907.

Kendall, Calvin N., and George A. Mirick. *How to Teach the Fundamental Subjects*. Boston: Houghton Mifflin, 1915.

Kennedy, Joseph. *Rural Life and the Rural School*. New York: American Book Co., 1915.

Kerr, Clark. *The Uses of the University*. 5th ed. Cambridge: Harvard University Press, 2001.

King, Carlyle. *Extending the Boundaries: Scholarship and Research at the University of Saskatchewan, 1909–1966*. Saskatoon: University of Saskatchewan, 1967.

Kingdon, John W. *Agendas, Alternatives, and Public Policies*. 2nd ed. New York: Harper Collins, 1995.

Kliebard, Herbert M. *The Struggle for the American Curriculum, 1893–1958*. New York: Routledge, 1995.

Lagemann, Ellen Condliffe. *An Elusive Science: The Troubling History of Education Research*. Chicago: University of Chicago Press, 2000.

Langley, Gerald James. "The Programs of Study Authorized for Use in the North-West Territories to 1905 and the Province of Saskatchewan to 1931, and the Text Books Prescribed in Connection Therewith." Master's thesis, University of Saskatchewan, 1944.

LaRue, Daniel Wolford. *The Science and the Art of Teaching*. New York: American Book Co., 1917.

Laycock, David. *Populism and Democratic Thought in the Canadian Prairies, 1910–1945*. Toronto: University of Toronto Press, 1990.

Lears, Jackson. *Rebirth of a Nation: The Making of Modern America, 1877–1920*. New York: Harper Perennial, 2010.

Levine, Arthur O. *The American College and the Culture of Aspiration, 1915–1940*. Ithaca, NY: Cornell University Press, 1987.

Limerick, Patricia Nelson. *Something in the Soil: Legacies and Reckonings in the New West*. New York: W.W. Norton, 2000.

Link, William. *The Paradox of Southern Progressivism, 1880–1930*. Chapel Hill: UNC Press, 1997.

Lipset, Seymour Martin. *Agrarian Socialism: The Cooperative Commonwealth Federation in Saskatchewan (A Study in Political Sociology)*. Berkeley: University of California Press, 1971.

– *Continental Divide: The Values and Institutions of the United States and Canada*. New York: Routledge, 1999.

– *Revolution and Counterrevolution*. New York: Basic Books, Inc., 1968.

– "The Ideology of Local Control." In Bowers, Housego, and Dyke, eds., *Education and Social Policy*, 21–42.

Lloyd, Harry, and Richard T. Hargreaves. *The Self-Directed School*. New York: Charles Scribner's Sons, 1925.

Lyons, John. "Professional Decision Making and Educational Reform: The Saskatchewan Tradition." In Cochrane, ed., *So Much*, 16–36.

MacEwan, Grant. *Harvest of Bread*. Saskatoon: Prairie Books, 1969.

Marx, Leo. *The Machine in the Garden: Technology and the Pastoral Ideal in America*. New York: Oxford University Press, 2000.

McGerr, Michael. *The Rise and Fall of the Progressive Movement in America, 1870–1920*. New York: Free Press, 2003.

McInnis, Edgar. *Canada: A Political and Social History*. 3rd ed. Toronto: Holt Rinehart, 1969.

Milner, Cameron. "Valley Christian Academy: Promoting Diversity and Assimilation." In Brian Noonan, Dianne Hallman, and Murray Scharf, eds., *A History of Education in Saskatchewan: Selected Readings*, 109–24. Regina: Canadian Plains Research Centre, 2006.

Morton, Arthur S. *Saskatchewan: The Making of a University*. Toronto: University of Toronto Press, 1959.

Morton, W.L. *The Progressive Party in Canada*. Toronto: University of Toronto Press, 1967.

Murray, David R., and Robert A. Murray. *The Prairie Builder: Walter Murray of Saskatchewan*. Edmonton: NeWest Press, 1984.

Murray, Walter C. "History of Education in Saskatchewan." In Shortt and Doughty, eds., *Canada and Its Provinces*, 451–73.

Nasaw, David. *Schooled to Order: A Social History of Public Schooling in the United States*. New York: Oxford University Press, 1979.

Noonan, Brian. "Saskatchewan Separate Schools." In Brian Noonan, Dianne Hallman, and Murray Scharf, eds., *A History of Education in Saskatchewan: Selected Readings*, 21–32. Regina: Canadian Plains Research Centre, 2006.

Ohles, Frederik, Shirley M. Ohles, and John G. Ramsay. *Biographical Dictionary of Modern American Education*. Westport, Conn.: Greenwood Press, 1997.

Owen, Michael. "Towards a New Day: The Larger School Unit in Saskatchewan, 1935–1950." In Brian Noonan, Dianne Hallman, and Murray Scharf, eds., *A History of Education in Saskatchewan: Selected Readings*, 33–49. Regina: Canadian Plains Research Centre, 2006.

Owram, Doug. *Promise of Eden: The Canadian Expansionist Movement and Idea of the West, 1856–1900*. Toronto: University of Toronto Press, 1980.

Patterson, Robert S. "Progressive Education: Impetus to Educational Change in Alberta and Saskatchewan." In E. Brian Titley and Peter J. Miller, eds., *Education in Canada: An Interpretation*, 169–96. Calgary: Detselig Enterprises, 1982.

– "Society and Education during the Wars and Their Interlude: 1914–1945." In Wilson, Stamp, and Audet, eds., *Canadian Education*, 360–82.

Pells, Richard. *Not Like Us: How Europeans Have Loved, Hated, and Transformed American Culture since World War II*. New York: Basic Books, 1997.

Postel, Charles. *The Populist Vision*. New York: Oxford University Press, 2009.

Prentice, Alison. "The American Example." In Wilson, Stamp, and ·Audet, eds., *Canadian Education*, 41–68.

Prown, Jules David, et al. *Discovered Land, Invented Pasts: Transforming Views of the American West*. New Haven, Conn.: Yale University Press, 1994.

Putnam, Daniel. *Manual of Pedagogics*. New York: Silver, Burdett, and Co., 1895.

Raban, Jonathan, *Bad Land: An American Romance*. New York: Vintage Books, 1996.

Riley, Dylan. "The Historical Logic of *Logics of History*: Language and Labor in William H. Sewell Jr." *Social Science History* 32 no. 4 (winter 2008): 555–65.

Rodgers, Daniel T. *Atlantic Crossings: Social Politics in a Political Age*. Cambridge, Mass: Belknap Press, 1998.

Rorty, Richard. *Consequences of Pragmatism: Essays, 1972–1980*. Minneapolis: University of Minnesota Press, 1982.

– *Philosophy and Social Hope*. New York: Penguin Books, 1999.

– *Philosophy and the Mirror of Nature*. Princeton, NJ: Princeton University Press, 1979.

Ross, Peter N. "The Establishment of the Ph.D. at Toronto: A Case of American Influence." *History of Education Quarterly* (fall 1972): 358–80.

Rudolph, Frederick. *The American College and University: A History*. Athens: University of Georgia Press, 1990.

Scharf, M.P. "An Historical Overview of the Organization of Education in Saskatchewan." In Brian Noonan, Dianne Hallman, and Murray Scharf, eds., *A History of Education in Saskatchewan: Selected Readings*, 3–19. Regina: Canadian Plains Research Centre, 2006.

Second Book of The Alexandra Readers. Toronto: Macmillan Company of Canada, 1908.

Sewell, William H., Jr. "The Concept(s) of Culture." In Victoria E. Bonnell and Lynn Hunt, eds., *Beyond the Cultural Turn: New Directions in the Study of Society and Culture*, 35–61. Berkeley: University of California Press, 1999.

– *Work and Revolution in France: The Language of Labor from the Old*

Regime to 1848. New York: Cambridge University Press, 1980.

Sharp, Paul F. *The Agrarian Revolt in Western Canada: A Survey Showing American Parallels.* Winnipeg: Hignell Printing, 1997.

– *Whoop-Up Country: The Canadian-American West, 1865–1885.* Minneapolis: University of Minnesota Press, 1955.

Sheehan, Nancy. "A History of Higher Education in Canada." *Canadian Journal of Higher Education* 15 no. 1 (winter 1985): 25–38.

– "Character Training and the Cultural Heritage: An Historical Comparison of Canadian Elementary Readers." In G.S. Tomkins, ed., *The Curriculum in Canada in Historical Prspective,* 77–88. Edmonton: Canadian Society for the Study of Education, 1979.

Shepard, Robert Bruce. "American Influence on the Settlement and Development of the Canadian Plains." Unpublished dissertation, University of Regina, 1994.

Shortt, Adam, and Arthur G. Doughty. *Canada and Its Provinces.* Toronto: Glasgow, Brook & Company, 1914.

Slotkin, Richard. *Gunfighter Nation: The Myth of the Frontier in Twentieth-Century America.* Norman: University of Oklahoma Press, 1992.

– *Regeneration through Violence: The Mythology of the American Frontier, 1600–1860.* Norman: University of Oklahoma Press, 1972.

Smith, Henry Nash. *Virgin Land: The American West as Symbol and Myth.* Cambridge, Mass.: Harvard University Press, 1970.

Stamp, Robert M. "Education and the Economic and Social Milieu: The English Canadian Scene from the 1870s to 1914." In Wilson, Stamp, and Audet, eds., *Canadian Education,* 314–36.

Steffes, Tracy L. "Solving the 'Rural School Problem': New State Aid, Standards, and Supervision of Local Schools 1900–1933." *History of Education Quarterly* 48 no. 2 (May 2008): 181–220.

Stegner, Wallace. *Wolf Willow: A History, a Story, and a Memory of the Last Plains Frontier.* New York: Penguin Books, 2000.

Stevenson, Garth. *Unfulfilled Union: Canadian Federalism and National Unity.* Toronto: Macmillan, 1979.

Strayer, George Drayton. *A Brief Course in the Teaching Process.* New York: MacMillan, 1920.

Sutherland, Neil. "The 'New' Education in Anglophone Canada: 'Modernization' Transforms the Curriculum." In *The Curriculum in*

Canada in Historical Perspective, CSSE Yearbook, 49–59. Vancouver: Canadian Society for the Study of Education, 1979.

Thacker, Robert, "Introduction: No Catlin without Kane; or, *Really Understanding the 'American' West.*" In Higham and Thacker, eds., *One West, Two Myths II*, 1–11.

Thelin, John R. *A History of American Higher Education*. Baltimore: Johns Hopkins University Press, 2004.

Thorndike, Edward L. *Principles of Teaching Based on Psychology*. New York: A.G. Seiler, 1916.

Titley, E. Brian, and Peter J. Miller, eds. *Education in Canada: An Interpretation*. Calgary: Detselig Enterprises, 1982.

Tomkins, George S. "Canadian Education and the Development of a National Consciousness." In Alf Chaiton and Neil McDonald, eds., *Canadian Schools and Canadian Identity*, 6–28. Toronto: Gage, 1976.

– *A Common Countenance: Stability and Change in the Canadian Curriculum*. Scarborough, Ont.: Prentice Hall, 1986.

– "Foreign Influences on Curriculum and Curriculum Policy Making in Canada: Some Impressions in Historical and Contemporary Perspective." *Curriculum Inquiry* 11 no. 2 (1981): 157–66.

Turner, Frederick Jackson. *The Frontier in American History*. New York: Dover, 1996.

Tyack, David B. *The One Best System: A History of American Urban Education*. Cambridge, Mass.: Harvard University Press, 1974.

Tyack, David B., and Larry Cuban. *Tinkering toward Utopia: A Century of Public School Reform*. Cambridge, Mass.: Harvard University Press, 1995.

Veysey, Lawrence R. *The Emergence of the American University*. Chicago: University of Chicago Press, 1970.

Von Heyking, Amy. *Creating Citizens: History and Identity in Alberta's Schools, 1905 to 1980*. Calgary: University of Calgary Press, 2006.

Waiser, Bill. *Saskatchewan: A New History*. Calgary: Fifth House, 2005.

Webb, Prescott. *The Great Plains*. Lincoln: University of Nebraska Press, 1981.

White, Richard. *"It's Your Misfortune and None of My Own": A New History of the American West*. Norman: University of Oklahoma Press, 1991.

– *Railroaded: The Transcontinentals and the Making of Modern America*.

New York: W.W. Norton, 2011.

Widdis, Randy William. "Borderland Interaction in the International Region of the Great Plains: An Historic-Geographical Perspective." *Great Plains Research* 7 (spring 1997): 103–37.

Wiebe, Robert H. *The Search for Order, 1877–1920*. New York: Hill and Wang, 1967.

Wilson, J. Donald. "Education in Upper Canada: Sixty Years of Change." In Wilson, Stamp, and Audet, eds., *Canadian Education*, 190–213.

– "The Ryerson Years in Canada West." In Wilson, Stamp, and Audet, eds., *Canadian Education*, 214–40.

Wilson, J. Donald, Robert M. Stamp, and Louis Philippe-Audet, eds. *Canadian Education: A History*. Scarborough, Ont.: Prentice Hall, 1970.

Wiseman, Nelson. "The Pattern of Prairie Politics." In Francis and Palmer, eds., *The Prairie West*, 640–60.

Wolfe, Alan. "The Missing Pragmatic Revival in American Social Science." In Morris Dickstein, ed., *The Revival of Pragmatism: New Essays in Social Thought, Law, and Culture*, 199–206. Durham, NC: Duke University Press, 1998.

Wood, Louis Aubrey. *A History of Farmer's Movements in Canada*. Toronto: Ryerson Press, 1924.

Worster, Daniel. *Under Western Skies: Nature and History in the American West*. New York: Oxford University Press, 1992.

Worster, Donald: "Two Faces West: The Development Myth in Canada and the United States." In Higham and Thacker, eds., *One West, Two Myths II*, 23–45.

Zilverschmit, Arthur. *Changing Schools: Progressive Education Theory and Practice, 1930–1960*. Chicago: University of Chicago Press, 1993.

Index

east, representations of, in west, 46–8
east-to-west axis, 25, 52
education policy: in Ontario, 24
Elazar, Daniel J.: on individualistic sub-culture, 82; on moralistic sub-culture, 13, 29, 43, 79, 81–2, 98, 143, 157; on political culture, 27; on traditionalistic sub-culture, 82
Evans, Sterling, 34
expert: role of 146, 149, 154; US expert in Saskatchewan, 7, 38–41, 87, 92, 97–9, 105, 109–10

faculty members, US-trained, at University of Saskatchewan, 8
Falconer, Sir Robert, 135
farm machinery: US–made in Saskatchewan, 33–4
Foght, Harold W., 17, 75, 92–116, 143, 147, 150–3, 167; *The American Rural School*, 99, 102; anti-eastern stance, 97, 111; anti-urban stance, 96, 110, 111, 144; populist thought, 94; rural emphasis, 96; *Rural Denmark and Its Schools*, 96; *Rural School Consolidation in Missouri*, 96; *Survey of Saskatchewan Education*, 18, 40–1, 73, 76, 107, 108, 112
forty-ninth parallel, 11, 13, 167
Francis, R. Douglas, 166
Friesen, Gerald, 59
frontier, 48, 58; US, 9, 24, 26

frontier thesis. *See* Turner, Frederick Jackson
Funk, Jack, 94, 152, 154

Gast, John, *American Progress*, 54–5
GI Bill (US), 164
graduate education: Saskatchewanians in United States, 7, 37–8, 74
Grange, 32
Great Plains, US, 16, 52. *See also* continental plains
Greenway, S.E., 132

Hall, G. Stanley, 71
Halleck, Rueben Post, *Psychology and Psychic Culture*, 72
Hallman, Diane, 88
Hanus, Paul, 40
Hardy, Evan, 126–7
Haultain, F.W.G., 79, 122
Hayden, Michael, 124, 135
Herbart, Johann Friedrich, 71
Herzberg, Gerhard, 131
Higham and Thacker, *One West, Two Myths*, 2 volumes, 166–7
higher education: in Saskatchewan, 12; Saskatchewanian's pursuit of, in the United States, 37–8
Hill, A.R., University of Missouri, 125–6, 136
hinterland, 12, 13
hinterland/metropolis. *See* Innis, Harold

Slotkin, Richard, 48, 140
Smith, Henry Nash, 54
Social Credit Party in Alberta, 44
social efficiency approach to
    school reform, 24, 38, 98,
    101, 107–46, 147, 149, 163: and
    science, 111, and universities, 139
"sociological tour," 33–6, 75–8,
    175–6n23
Stamp, Robert M., 93
Stegner, Wallace, *Wolf Willow*, 90,
    168
Stevenson, Garth, 152
Story of the Canadian People, The,
    85
Strachan, John, 23

textbooks: from Ontario, 7; from
    the United States, 7, 23
Thacker, Robert, 168
Thelin, John, 123, 129
third parties: in Alberta, 44; in
    Canada, 44; in Saskatchewan,
    44; in the United States, 44
Thompson, James, 134
Thorndike, Edward, 72, 114
Thorvaldson Building, University
    of Saskatchewan, 123
Tomkins, George S., 6, 72, and *A
    Common Countenance*, 6, 21
traditionalistic political sub-
    culture, 82
transportation of rural students,
    108
Turner, Frederick Jackson, 30–1,
    48, 166–8

Twiss, Fannie A., 76–7
Tyack and Cuban, 98, 107
Tyack, David, 40, 146; *One Best
    System*, 101, 153

universities: corporate-like
    structure, 119, 124–8; in eastern
    Canada, 122
University of Alberta, 130
University of Chicago, 37, 74, 85–6
university faculty, 120; at
    University of Saskatchewan,
    124, 132
university president: role of, 124
University of Manitoba, 130
University of Saskatchewan, 7,
    17; College of Agriculture,
    17, 126, 135, 138–40, 159, 164;
    corporate structure of, 28;
    extension program, 126, 138,
    159, 160; sociological tours, 127;
    US philanthropy to, 128–32,
    140–1; vocationalism at, 138–9;
    Wisconsin Idea at, 134–41, 164
University of Toronto, 125
urban/rural comparison,
    Saskatchewan, 17, 18
US culture: influence on
    Saskatchewan, 8, 25–61
US education practice in
    Saskatchewan, 65–74, 79
US faculty members at University
    of Saskatchewan, US models
    for teacher training, 70–4
US Plains organizations in
    Saskatchewan, 31–3

US political culture in Saskatchewan, 42–61
US popular culture in Saskatchewan, 36
US publications in Saskatchewan, 32–3
US settlers: Alberta and Saskatchewan, 9; US origin of, 9, 28–31
US settlers in Saskatchewan, difficulty in identifying, 19–22, 28–9
US student readers in Saskatchewan, 79–85
US-trained teachers: in Saskatchewan, 7, 67–70

Van Hise, Charles, 159
Van Horne, William C., 40
vernacular architecture, 40
Veteran's Rehabilitation Act (VRA), Canada, 164
Veysey, Lawrence, 118–19, 124, 134
vocational education, 75–144, 145; and US models of, 76, 92, 102, 103, 111, 112, 160, 163
Vocational Education Act, 1920 (Saskatchewan), 113
vocational program within universities: criticism of, 120, 160
vocational university, 119, 159

Waiser, Bill: on US-born people in Saskatchewan, 21, 28
Washburne, Dr Carlton, 77–8

Washington University, St Louis, MO, 8, 123, 124
"waste" in schools, 110, 114
Webb, Walter Prescott, 48–52; as continentalist, 11
west: American, 54–5; anti-eastern sentiment, 19, 45; Canadian, 42; relative to the east, 46–55; shared meanings of, 45–61, 70, 165–6; symbols of, 54–9
western perceptions of the east: in Canada, 42; in the United States, 54–5
Western Producer (Turner's Weekly), 32, 39, 40, 46–8
Wheeler, Seager, 34
Wheeler's Graded Literary Readers, 84
White, Richard, 52, 166
Widdis, Randy, 29
Winnetka Plan, 77–8, 89, 116
"Wisconsin Idea," 8, 134–9, 159
Wolfe, Alan, 10
Worster, Donald, 166

Young and Field Literary Reader, The, 84